DON'T WRITE ME OFF!
THIRTY-NINE STORIES OF OLDER ADULTHOOD

JEWISH SENIOR LIFE OF METROPOLITAN DETROIT

CONTENTS

Foreword	vii
Introduction	xi
I'M FINE Arthur Lipsitt (of blessed memory)	1
GETTING OLD WITHOUT REGRET Regina Amromin	3
A TRAVELIN' MAN Larry Aronoff	7
THERE'S ONLY ONE ADA BANDALENE! Ada Bandalene	9
THE SOUNDS OF MUSIC Shirley Benyas	14
RECREATING A LIFE Edith Birnholtz	17
UNEXPECTED LAUGHTER Edie Blumer	21
96 AND STILL VOLUNTEERING Rose Cooper	25
MY BEST FRIENDS Audrey Demak	28
BITTER/SWEET Marilyn Dizik	31
THE SOUNDS AROUND ME Harry Doren	35
TICK TOCK Toni Fontana	38
FINDING CONTENTMENT Shmuel Graybar	43
A NIGHT AT THE CATSKILLS Harriet Hessenthaler	45
BETTER PLANS Bonnie Hubert, CNA, HHA	48

MY TWO PASSIONS Eleanor Johnson	52
THE FAMILY MAN Bernie Jonas	55
CANCER IS A PAIN IN THE BUTT! Nancy Kalef	58
THE YELLOW BOX Ruth Katz	62
FREEDOM Harriet Kovacs	65
NOTES FROM MY LIFE Harry Krim	70
CHOOSING GRATITUDE Ruthe Levy	73
IF THERE'S A WILL, THERE'S A WAY Phyllis Lewkowicz	77
KINDERTRANSPORT Edith Maniker	82
IT'S NOT RIGHT TO BURY A CHILD Carole Master	85
A SEA OF SUPPORT Debbie Merin	91
ONE AND BE DONE Jill Messinger	94
A LOOK IN THE MIRROR Adele Nodler	99
TIMOTHY Diane Pliskow	103
THE WORLD: MY OYSTER Roz Rogers	106
GRANDMA DOHERTY Ilene Rubin	109
FLY GIRL Terri Silberstein	112
THE GIFT OF ART Ann Spencer	115
TINY TREASURES Ann Torf	118

MOVED BY THE WORD OF G-D Regina Turner	121
HOW I MET MY HUSBAND Debbie Warner	124
MY FRIEND'S FRIENDSHIP WITH HASHEM Laura M. Watson	127
GETTING BACK UP Sheba Zietchick	130
FITNESS, BODY AND SOUL Millie Friedman Zivov	132
THE GREAT WHITE HUNTER Al Zlatkin	136
Acknowledgments	139
Creative Team	141
Jewish Senior Life of Metropolitan Detroit	147

FOREWORD
DON'T WRITE THESE PEOPLE OFF (OR ANY PEOPLE, COME TO THINK OF IT)

What would we be if not for our stories?

Much poorer folks, for sure.

At a stage in life when so many women and men look back on bygone days and reflect in misty reverie, the authors in these pages took a path less traveled. They have shared with us their much more recent experiences, some quite unusual for seniors. They tell of broadened horizons, challenges met and conquered, opportunities seized, and bucket list items finally checked off.

Some stories are frankly eye-opening in their lack of inhibition; several are poignant and touching; a goodly number are strange but true; and more than a few are preposterously funny. The deft hands of the editors have woven threads of stark simplicity and refreshing candor into a colorful tapestry of lives lived well in the twilight years.

Page after page rewards the reader with the relevant and unexpected, offering insight into what it means to be vitally and vibrantly alive at an "advanced" age. Especially so in a society so smitten with youth it can't be bothered to respect — let alone revere — the sagacity of its seniors.

There are reasons for that. Not good reasons and not excuses, but reasons.

In this age of information, we are pummeled almost into submission by breathless breaking news, compounded by mind-numbing data and statistics. As if that weren't enough, we get dose after dose of interpretation, analysis, and commentary from those omnipresent talking heads who so often seem to know everything and understand nothing. No surprise, then, to feel we have seen and heard it all — and not just once, but again and again.

For six and a half decades, my chosen trade has been as a writer and a publisher. I'm an advocate for communication, but I must confess, I'm starting to think, *Enough already.*

But not entirely.

That's because this book stands as evidence that something vital has been buried beneath that flood of commentary. It is uncommon these days to come upon a story offering a meaningful glimpse into what it means to be a human being.

That is why this book is meaningful. That is why books such as this have special significance at this moment in this society. My infallible crystal ball tells me that this era in which we live will not be looked upon with favor by future civilizations. Our time here will be regarded not so much for what we have created but for what we have wasted. In that litany of losses, I would put at the top rank how we failed to exploit the resources and the experiences — and yes, the personal stories — of our seniors.

Collectively, the seemingly small stories in this book eloquently tell the Big Story. And what is that Big Story? It is that we let lie fallow the powers and the passions of our nation's elders at our own peril.

For six decades, I have urged government officials to take meaningful action on tapping the wealth of experience, resources, and, surely, the reserves of energy of our nation's seniors. My letters and emails have landed in baskets from the White House to the halls of Congress. I do not complain that I have been ignored. To the contrary: I have gotten expressions of agreement, hear-hear, and atta-boy. I have yet to hear disagreement. I have also yet to see action.

I don't know it all, for sure, but I do know this:

The world would be the lesser if real stories such as these were not captured for posterity. And therein lies a lesson, a challenge, and a threat.

This book has a modest goal and a brilliant title. *Don't Write Me Off!* perfectly sums up not just this book, but, by coincidence, the plea I've been making to governments since the 1960s to unleash the pent-up potency of our nation's seniors — and most especially, by the way, of women.

That is why I am so pleased that these editors have gathered, orchestrated, polished, and preserved this collection. These are stories of this particular time and this particular place by these undaunted authors. Imagine the countless similar stories that will go untold, unremarked. Imagine what could be accomplished in so many other domains — climate, health, industry, business, the arts — if we put a national priority on mining the resources locked within our nation's seniors.

Not solely in personal stories like these, of course, as revealing as they are of the human spirit, but in so many other ways. In the truly priceless experiences of senior women and men in the vocations and callings that occupied them in their working lives.

Our seniors bring much more than a recitation of triumphs and successes; they embody dearly earned lessons from mistakes they made. These lessons learned could and should be exploited and built upon and those mistakes avoided by succeeding generations.

Granted, those lessons are not to be found in these pages. But the accounts of what these men and women took on in just their last few years might give a sense of what they could still offer to those in the occupations and activities they pursued before retirement.

In these pages, we are transported from the depths of sorrow when losing a child to the lofty thrill of skydiving. We share in the satisfaction of having a new companion in life — whether a cat, dog, or a significant other. Through the words of these authors, we feel what it means to be at a stage of life during which you continue to feel palpably the highs, the lows, and just about everything in between.

Through the eyes and lives of these authors, we see that the most savored experience of all is the next one.

Bill Haney
Writer, editor, publisher, and author of *What They Were Thinking: Reflections on Michigan Difference-Makers*

INTRODUCTION

My grandfather used to say, "growing old isn't for sissies." And my experience at Jewish Senior Life has borne that out. There are no sissies here. There are all kinds of people, of many ages and in all kinds of physical condition, but not one sissy. In fact, I've found this to be a rather tough group. They do what they want, say what they mean, and, man, they know stuff! They have memories and perspectives and the time to sit and share them in a meaningful way.

This book was born out of my experience getting to know the residents at JSL. I enjoyed it so much; I figured readers would too. The following is a collection of their thoughts, stories, recollections, poems, and mottos — a chorus of older voices sharing their lives.

And it's not just the past they're sharing. There's plenty of present. We chose to call the book *Don't Write Me Off!* not just because it's punny, but because, in our culture, we do write off older people. As I'm leaving middle age and entering my own third act, I've started to experience just how much gray hair renders one mute, invisible.

I invented a new term for it I call "kidsplaining" — well,

maybe I didn't invent it, but I'm giving myself credit for it — and you won't find any of it in this book (unless I still count).

This isn't a book about aging well, about running marathons or getting college degrees at 80 and 90. It's about the stuff that really makes us tough: life experience and what we learn from it. Everyone in this book has survived something and found life, love, friendship, and new passions waiting on the other side.

There are 39 stories in this book and through the process of putting it together, I have come to admire and adore each and every one of its writers. I hope you will too.

Beth Robinson
Director of FRIENDS of Jewish Senior Life

I'M FINE
ARTHUR LIPSITT (OF BLESSED MEMORY)

There's nothing whatever the matter with me.
I'm just as healthy as I can be.
I have arthritis in both my knees
And when I talk, I talk with a wheeze.
My pulse is weak and my blood is thin.
But I'm awfully well for the shape I'm in.

I think my liver is out of whack
And a terrible pain is in my back.
My hearing is poor, my sight is dim
Most everything seems to be out of trim
But I'm awfully well for the shape I'm in.

I have arch supports for both my feet
Or I wouldn't be able to go on the street.
Sleeplessness I have, night after night
And in the morning, I'm just a sight.
My memory is failing. My head's in a spin.
I'm peacefully living on aspirin,
But I'm awfully well for the shape I'm in.

2 ARTHUR LIPSITT (OF BLESSED MEMORY)

> *The moral is, as the tale we unfold*
> *That for you and me who are growing old*
> *It's better to say, "I'm fine," with a grin*
> *Than to let them know the shape we're in.*

Arthur Lipsitt (of blessed memory), was a poet, former Jewish Senior Life resident, and 8 Over 80 Tikkun Olam Award recipient.

GETTING OLD WITHOUT REGRET
REGINA AMROMIN

People say, "Getting old is not fun!" Maybe there is some truth in it: getting tired quickly, having all kinds of aches and pains, vision declining, and sometimes the hearing too. These limitations usually accompany us in old age, upsetting us and making us sigh.

But there is another expression, widely known in Russia: "My years are my wealth." Our experiences, professional accomplishments, discretion, freedom from the thoughtlessness and impetuousness of youth, our love for our children and grandchildren, and our opportunity to provide them with advice, support, and help.

The feeling of being needed is precious! It comes to us over the years and is most valuable in old age, at least for me. I am getting old. The process started when I retired, but I like noticing positive changes in my character and behavior, and I believe this is a common feeling for people over 60.

I am getting old without any regrets. And besides all the advantages of being old, I have my own reasons for gratitude.

First was my move with my family to the United States from Russia in 2002. I was already retired then. Of course, during the first several years, it took great effort to adapt to a new country. I had to work a lot and go to college to learn English. But the move to the USA provided me a level of wellbeing and peace of mind which allowed me to age without regret.

In comparison to life in the USA, the life of retirees in Russia is very difficult, financially and emotionally. In the best-case scenario, retired elders are needed by their family members, despite being seen as burdens by the state and society. Russian social security and medical organizations try to brush the elderly off and avoid solving their problems.

Second, both my old and new hobbies and favorite activities bring me joy and positive emotions. Now, I have time for them — not only for activities, but also to enjoy their results.

One of my hobbies is fishing, which I have loved since my

childhood. I like sitting by the water with a fishing rod, enjoying the beauty and sounds of nature and later, if I am lucky, enjoying my own cooked fish for dinner.

Another hobby I have developed in America is cooking. In Russia, cooking was an obligation. Our family was large — seven people. On my way home from work, I often had to stand in long lines to get groceries. I had to cook not what I liked but what was quickest, with only the produce I was lucky to get. The choices in Russian stores were very limited then.

In America, everything changed. The abundance allows me to buy any kind of groceries, and I do not have to stand in lines. I have plenty of spare time, so I can find any recipe I want online and cook or bake something yummy and interesting to treat my children and grandchildren. I am in the kitchen very often these days, cooking different hot and cold meals, making drinks, and baking pastries, torts, cakes, and cookies. This is my new hobby.

I have also started socializing online, and I have made friends with a very nice Ukrainian family, a friendship we've shared for more than three years.

In 2003, my niece, who lives here in Michigan, had a baby on the same day as my dad's birthday. The baby boy was named after him. I spent a lot of time babysitting little Aron, and for my dad's 100th birthday anniversary, I made a picture album to tell him about his great-grandfather's life story and his namesake.

My father lived a very interesting and successful life. He was also a very good storyteller, and we children loved listening to his stories. My work on the photo album grew into a book I wrote about my father; thus, another hobby — writing — entered my life.

After finishing the memoir, I started researching the genealogy of my family, and I wrote a book: *The Notes on Genealogy*. Writing it took a significant amount of time on the internet. I think this book will be useful and interesting for my children and grandchildren, because it tells the story of six generations of our family on both my father and mother's sides.

This awakened the urge to write a memoir of my own life. There are 200 pages in the book, which I finished I in 2022. *My Life in Stories and Reflections* covers episodes throughout my life and my thoughts about times and events in my country and the world at large, as it all greatly influenced the formation of my worldview and the destiny of my family.

I like writing poetry as well. I am gradually accumulating my poems into another book, *Poetic Experience*. It will be part of my legacy for my children and grandchildren.

So, my aging is full of different passions, hobbies, and creativity. It does not leave any time for deficiencies of age. Yes, sometimes I get sick and sometimes I feel sad, but that's life, and swings of mood are inevitable at any age. But there are also special and nice things one only gets to enjoy in older age.

Let's not be afraid of the word "aging." Yes, I am an older person. I am 77. I am a grandmother and a great-grandmother, but I am happy in my aging. I am truly getting old without regret.

Regina, 77, was born in Saint Petersburg (Leningrad), Russia. She was a teacher and high school vice principal. She lives at Prentis Apartments. She has three children, Vera, Anatoliy, and Yuriy; eight grandchildren, Pavel, Devin, Dominik, Emily, Sophia, Aiden, Valerie, and Nikolay; and one great-grandson, Maxim. She likes fishing, cooking, and communicating on the internet, and writes poetry and memoirs, creating keepsake books for her children and grandchildren.

A TRAVELIN' MAN
LARRY ARONOFF

If I were to choose something to be remembered by, it would be my love of travel.

Many of my most memorable trips were with family, since family is and always has been especially important to me. One vacation that stands out was to Israel in 2017; this first visit to the promised land made a lasting impression.

"Active" trips were a big part of our family plans. Skiing in Colorado with the kids was fantastic. Touring England was both educational and fun. Sailing to the Caribbean area — St. Martin and the British Virgin Islands — was the best.

At one time, if you were to ask me about my favorite song, I might have said "Sailing, Sailing (Over the Bounding Main)." Not because I was a great singer, but because this described my greatest passion: sailing my own vessel. For 50 years I was a member of the Great Lakes Yacht Club, and for one year I was commodore, running the club.

Sailing my craft on vacations, such as to the North Channel in Canada, always made for a lovely adventure. We docked at several islands that are quite isolated. Ahh, the peaceful quiet!

When I think in terms of a life well-lived, I put a lot of emphasis on staying active. The local Y sees me three days a week for swimming and two days for working out, lifting weights, etc. Senior residence living — social events and socializing — fills the rest of my days.

Larry Aronoff, 86, lives at Hechtman Apartments. He was born in Detroit and ran a medical supply business for 55 years. He has four children and six grandchildren.

THERE'S ONLY ONE ADA BANDALENE!
ADA BANDALENE

I used to live in the Knightsbridge area with my husband Kal. It was a lovely, charming house, a very big house with spacious living areas and three bedrooms and bathrooms. We had a wonderful walking trail nearby, and every day, I used to walk on it with my neighbors and friends. It was a lovely lifestyle.

When my husband passed away 11 years ago, I was still working. I taught exercise classes at Fleischman, where I met a lot of interesting people. Fleischman was a place for people who needed help, and I would come in and offer my assistance.

I worked to give them what they needed, whether they were in a wheelchair or using a walker. I always emphasized safety: "Bob, pull your wheelchair up. I don't want you standing. Use your upper body and arms and legs as much as you can, but no dancing when we stand." I aimed to empower them, reminding them that we all know how to breathe, take our heart rate, and sense when we feel well or unwell.

I volunteered at Fleischman for about 12 years, working with wonderful people like Carol Rosenberg and Barbara Giles. I even worked with the memory care patients on the third floor. That was a challenge to me, because sometimes it wasn't fun. It was an exercise class, but we would sing songs, sometimes; they all knew "Que Sera, Sera" by Doris Day.

I always tried to make everything fun, even if it wasn't. I said "good for you" to let them know they were doing a good job. Some of them couldn't talk, but as they left in their wheelchairs, they would grab my hand and give it a loving squeeze, a kind of *Thank you, I hope to see you next week.*

After volunteering, I would go back home. I was still in Knightsbridge, and I found I was always looking forward to leaving the house. With so much space, I found myself getting lonely after my husband's passing. I tried to stay busy, going out to lunch with friends and attending activities at Temple Shir

Shalom, though I eventually stopped going to Friday evening services due to transportation issues.

My son, Stuart, convinced me to check out Meer. He knew about the various programs available there and had friends whose parents lived there. He knows as many people here as I do.

When I walked through Meer for the first time, I met various people, like Marcia, in the hallway who asked if I was coming here. I wasn't entirely sure if I belonged, but as I learned more about the programs and activities, I began to see the appeal. It reminded me of the camp experiences that had brought so much joy to my life.

My journey to camp started when I worked at an ice cream place called The Zukins when I was around 13 or 14. Every Friday night, we hosted a talent show that brought the neighborhood together. During this time, a talent scout noticed me and asked if I was interested in singing or dancing in the USO. I agreed, but only if they could provide transportation, since I didn't have a car.

In the USO, I traveled to different bases, including Panama, where I performed pantomime and even tap-danced once, despite having no prior tap-dancing experience. I even performed a comedy act. It was all about bringing laughter and joy to servicemen and servicewomen.

My time at the USO shows introduced me to the likes of Frank Sinatra and Sammy Davis Jr. and fueled my dreams of becoming a movie star.

I was also a swimmer, and I used to work out at the Jewish center. Camp Tamakwa's famous Uncle Lou Handler (played by Alan Arkin in the movie *Indian Summer*) used to work out at the center, too, and he watched me swim. He stopped me one day and asked, "Would you like to come to camp?"

I said, "I've never been to camp, what am I going to do?"

And he said, "I'll show you what you're going to do."

So, we drove up to camp and he took me on the tour. It was

so big, I said, "Oh my G-d" — it was like the grounds here at Meer! They were big and had huge cabins and tennis courts, a girls' dock and a boys' dock.

"I could use you on the boys' dock," Uncle Lou said. And so I started working there.

On visiting day, I said, "Guys, we're going to have a water show — you know I have always wanted to be a movie star!" I thought I was Esther Williams. So, we did this water ballet. We did a water wheel where you hang onto the girl in front of you with your heels and take a deep breath and the water wheel goes underwater. You've got to hold your breath until you make that full circle, and so we worked on it and worked on it.

The boys' cabin used to watch us, and they went, "We can do that." It was like a comedy, what we did in the water. The girls were lovely wearing their floral hats, and when the boys did the water wheel, oh my G-d, they looked sloppy coming up — but the parents loved it. They applauded harder for the guys than they did for us.

But their praise was the most valuable reward. It meant more to me than any monetary reward.

Camp was a transformative time for me. It helped me overcome a difficult childhood and grow as an adult. It was therapeutic, making me stronger emotionally and mentally. I spent about 30 years working there. They had a song they would sing when I went into the dining hall — they would clap and stomp and sing "There's Only One Ada Bandalene."

Meer has all kinds of activities, just like camp. We celebrate holidays like Mother's Day, Father's Day, Veterans Day, and Flag Day with enthusiasm. I love dressing up for these occasions. It reminds me of my love for costumes and performing. We recently had a truly memorable "roaring '20s" event that honored the young folks serving in the dining room.

As I reflect on these experiences, I'm grateful for the ways they've shaped me and brought joy to my life. Whether it was teaching, performing, or volunteering, these moments have allowed me to connect with people, bring smiles to their faces, and, in turn, find happiness myself.

As I reflect on my life's journey, I can't help but appreciate how each phase, from my time at camp to my experiences with the USO, has contributed to the person I am today. These moments of connection, whether through teaching, performing, or simply sharing laughter, have been a source of immense happiness for me.

Now, in this new chapter of my life at Meer, I see the same potential for joy and connection. Somebody picked up the old camp song somewhere, and I recently went to a Meer event and was greeted with a rousing chorus of "There's Only One Ada Bandalene"!

Looking ahead, I eagerly anticipate the upcoming events and activities at Meer, such as the '50s day celebration. Just like in my camp days, I love dressing up for these events.

I have so much gratitude for the many moments, both big and small, that have shaped my life. From the laughter-filled days at camp to the stage performances for the troops, these experiences have made me who I am today: a person who finds purpose in bringing happiness to others. And now, as I embark on this new chapter at Meer, I look forward to creating more joyful memories and connecting with the wonderful people here.

Ada, 91, lives at Meer Apartments. Born in Detroit, she has worked as a physical education teacher and fitness instructor. She has three children, Stuart Bandalene, Linda Hough, and Amy Boros; eight grandchildren, Connor, Allison, Elana, Ryan, Alissa, Brianna, Leah, and Brendon; and one great-grandchild on the way. Ada likes to do everything, particularly exercise and watch comedy and opinion shows. She loves the show Everybody Loves Raymond. *Ada was an 8 Over 80 Tikkun Olam Award recipient.*

THE SOUNDS OF MUSIC
SHIRLEY BENYAS

If I had to summarize my life in two words, they would be "music" and "family." It was my mother, a Polish immigrant, raised by a well-educated father, who introduced me to classical music and opera at an early age, and the music bug never left me.

My mother was my best friend. As I developed into an artist as a young woman, I made the choice to have a family of my own and raise my children rather than testing the waters of being a professional opera singer while spending little time at home.

Initially, my professional career was as a music teacher in the Detroit Public Schools for 31 years, educating other children during the day while raising my own at home. I always performed, singing excerpts from great operas, art songs, and other classical works with other professionals in the Detroit area. As my children grew up, and as my public-school teaching career waned, other performing opportunities opened up in musical theater — and as Michigan became a filmmaking destination, in that medium as well.

As a young woman, I studied theater under actress Uta Hagen and attended an opera workshop with Boris Goldovsky. I remember well doing scenes to learn the craft, as well as a performance as Mimi in *La Boheme*. That role did a lot to bring me out of myself; I was quite shy until that time. I did not just portray the tragic heroine; I really felt that I *was* Mimi, and the audience reaction to my performance affirmed that. Another early role was that of Olympia in *Tales of Hoffman*.

Locally, I appeared in roles in two productions of the Michigan Opera Theatre, in *My Fair Lady* and *Follies*. I was well into enjoying my craft, obviously.

As a resident at Meer, I have organized a reader's theater group, which has met with good reactions. At times, it was a struggle. One early production was just not going well, and the dress rehearsal was awful — but the actual performance went without a hitch. The performers were elated; the audience was most receptive.

I recall one man who was quite shy but who confessed to me after the show that he had really been able to come out of himself. He continued with the group for many years. I have since heard this from several participants, and that "news" is most rewarding.

Many happy memories are generated by recalling my teaching of a Yiddish class for those who heard it spoken at home and did not know what was being said.

My greatest joy now, however, comes from my children and talented grandchildren.

Shirley, 96, lives at Meer Apartments. She was married to photographer Bob Benyas (of blessed memory) for 63 years. She taught vocal music in the Detroit School System for 31 years and is a member of the Screen Actors Guild and the Actors' Equity Association. She has two sons, Mark Benyas and Eddie Benyas, and four grandchildren, Jordan, Dana, Gabriela, and Maya. Shirley was honored as an 8 Over 80 Tikkun Olam Award recipient.

RECREATING A LIFE
EDITH BIRNHOLTZ

It was Passover, 1944, and we were putting away the dishes in our home outside of Munkács when the Germans came for us. Munkács, pronounced *munkatsh*, was a part of former Czechoslovakia, now Ukraine, that was taken by Hungary in 1938.

The Germans took the residents of Munkács to work in a brick factory which had become a ghetto. After a few weeks, they sent us by cattle trains to Auschwitz. When we arrived at Auschwitz, I was separated from my parents and my brother. I survived the now-infamous Selection and wound up in a barracks with my two older sisters.

In the barracks, we lay 14 people on a wooden shelf. I lay there with my two sisters, crying, "I want my mother." My sisters watched over me, putting me in the middle, pinching my cheeks so I looked healthier, giving me their shoes so I looked taller. I was only 15 years old.

My older sister was in the hospital with pneumonia when they sent us to Bergen-Belsen. They dragged her out of the hospital and put her on the train anyway. It was raining and we were wet and freezing in the open boxcar. We were in that train for days and she died there, with me.

One day at Bergen-Belsen, someone came running and said they had seen an English tank. We were liberated by the English, and they fed us and took care of us and sent us to nearby Celle, Germany, where they put us on a train to Budapest. When I got there, I saw a Russian soldier who looked so familiar to me — it was my brother! He had survived! He couldn't believe that our older sister, who was the strong one, hadn't survived — and that I, the smallest who never ate anything, had. My other sister survived as well but with TB, which had a long-term impact on her health.

When I got to the US, I went to day school and night school to learn English. I met my husband on the bus going to work at the Sanders factory. We were teenagers, and he was just a couple of years older than me. I was single and living with an elderly couple where Jewish Social Services placed me. The couple loved my husband because the woman loved singing, and my husband had a beautiful voice.

The woman invited my brother and his wife for Thanksgiving when all of a sudden, her cousin comes from the kitchen with a glass of wine and says, "We're going to sing to Joe and Edith a mazel tov, because they just got engaged!" Which we had, the night before. They made us a big shower and they made our wedding; we had no money.

My husband was working painting signs in the basement. He was very talented. Not only was he a sign painter, but he was also an artist. He could paint anything you showed him. He even won first prize as a window trimmer at Northland. He trained as a cantor by taking lessons with older cantors, and eventually ended up being the cantor at Ahavas Achim Synagogue with Rabbi Arm and Rabbi Gorelick.

When he retired, we were living in Delray Beach, Florida, where we had a house, a clubhouse, and a tennis court. I played a lot of tennis — I even got to play with the Williams sisters! I won first place in a tournament there. I could still play tennis if I had someone to play with, but I do watch tennis any time it's on TV.

In 2017, my husband Joe got sick. We needed to be near family, so in January 2018, we moved back to Detroit. We moved to Hechtman Apartments in West Bloomfield. Joe had an apartment right next to mine and I had round-the-clock help for him. When I left to go to my apartment, he would beg me to stay. He passed away in 2019.

I have made a new and very special friend at Hechtman, Flora Kam. We have many of the same interests, especially walking and going to the fitness room. Flora and I are both proud that we raised very educated children. I think back on that, and I'm amazed that I could do it. I was very young. There isn't a day Flora and I don't talk. She's very interesting and a wonderful friend.

Recently, I attended a carnival at Danto. I won a big stuffed panda in the raffle. My great-granddaughter loved it, so I gave it to her. She was so happy, but her little sister wanted it, too — so she gave it to her! They're very sweet girls. I have children and their spouses, grandsons and their spouses, and great-granddaughters nearby. I also have grandchildren and great-grandchildren in Chicago, New York, and London.

I have a wonderful family and Flora, but it does get lonely at times. I miss my husband. I came here with him and lost him here. We were together for a long time, and we were very happy.

Edith Birnholtz, 94, lives at Hechtman Apartments. She has three children, nine grandchildren (one deceased), and seven great-grandchildren. She likes to exercise, walk, read, bake, and watch tennis.

UNEXPECTED LAUGHTER
EDIE BLUMER

My husband Nathan died in his sleep on Sunday, November 8, 2009, at age 91 in our home in Oak Park, Michigan.

The day before, we had celebrated the wedding anniversary of Ron and Sue, our son and his wife, who lived in Novi. We arrived home later than usual that evening, but we were both feeling fine. Nate went to bed soon after, but I stayed up to read in the den.

The next morning, Nathan decided to stay in bed a little longer. I put on my robe, washed up, went into the kitchen, and read the Sunday paper while eating breakfast. When I realized that some time had gone by and Nathan had not come for his breakfast, I went to see what the delay was. My husband was still in bed, so I said, "Isn't it time you got up?" When there was no response, I walked closer and realized he wasn't breathing.

I hurried to the phone on the other side of the bed and called 911. After I explained the problem to the operator, I was told to keep the line open and to get my husband on the floor so it would be easier for the EMTs to work on him. Without thinking this would be difficult, I did this after placing the phone on the floor. When the operator started giving me instructions to perform CPR, I pulled the phone closer and the plug pulled out of the wall. After reconnecting the phone, I didn't know what else to do, so I called my son and gave him the news.

A few minutes later there was a knock on the door, and there stood five policemen and two EMTs. The police had parked around my court of five homes and the ambulance was in my driveway. One officer stayed with me in the living room collecting information, while the other four went into the bedroom with the two EMTs.

There was another knock on the door and this time it was a neighbor. I thought he was there to find out what was happening, but no, I was mistaken. He was there to say that one of the patrol cars was on fire.

The officer in the living room ran out to get his fire extinguisher, grabbing things out of the car. It was his car; he had parked it over a pile of leaves that had been raked to the curb for pickup, and the heat of the catalytic converter had ignited them. I notified the other policemen and they all ran out to get their extinguishers as well. It reminded me of the Keystone Cops of long ago.

When the fire couldn't be put out, they called the fire department and two trucks came out. Eventually the fire was extinguished, but not before all the car's glass shattered, the tires burned, and the car was a complete loss. People were coming from all directions to see what was going on because there was a huge black plume in the sky. The bark of a nearby tree had turned black and a photographer from Fox TV was kneeling on the grass in the middle of the court taking pictures for the news that evening.

Then, the female EMT kneeled down in front of me to say how sorry they all were that they were unable to revive my husband, and they left. Ron and Sue arrived and then the funeral director. He wanted to see my husband's discharge papers from World War II, but I couldn't recall where they were, so he said to bring them in when I found them.

The next morning, I was somewhat calmer and remembered where the papers were. I called Ron, and he and Sue drove me to Ira Kaufman's. Ron parked in front of the doors, as there wasn't a service being conducted, and Sue and I walked inside. While we waited for the papers to be copied, the director came out of his office, put his hand on my shoulder, and said, "No disrespect to you, Mrs. Blumer, but when I came to your home yesterday and saw all those police cars and two fire engines, I thought, 'Oh my G-d, she killed her husband.'"

Well, Sue and I burst into laughter. When the discharge papers were returned, we walked out still laughing. When we returned to the car, Ron said, "This is the first time I've been at a funeral home and people came out laughing." That brought on more laughter, and when we told Ron what was said to me, he had a good laugh too.

We had a few days when we were quite sad, but I will always remember the laughter as well.

Edie, 98, has lived at Meer Apartments for 10 years. While a student at Detroit's Commerce High School, Edie kept the books at an automotive supply store. Later, she worked at the phone company, as a bookkeeper at an insurance agency, and as the office manager of the Baptist Children's Home. She has two sons, Lawrence Blumer and Ronald Blumer; three grandchildren Sara, Michelle, and Samantha; and six great-grandchildren, Lillian (Q), Lucas, Eliana, Colin, Tilly, and Charlie Esther.

Edie loves to travel. She is an avid reader and a prolific writer in Meer's Creative Writing Class. Edie is very active at Meer, serving as treasurer on the Meer Resident Council and the Meer Executive Board, as a greeter at events, and as a liaison for new Meer residents.

96 AND STILL VOLUNTEERING
ROSE COOPER

I am 96 years old. I have been a resident at Jewish Senior Life for many, many years. I started volunteering after closing my store, a Hallmark card shop, which I had for eight years.

I became a volunteer after hearing that Fleischman residents needed helpers, and a friend of mine saw me in the lobby and said, "You're coming with me." So, I was introduced to another new experience through JSL.

The boutique became my favorite volunteer project. There was always so much to do. I would go to the apparel shows for a day of meeting new people, the reps, who were showing their merchandise in their booths. We ordered clothing, purses, gloves, jewelry, and scarves from them to be shipped to us. When the orders came, they had to be unpacked, and we had to find the right spot in the store for them, which often meant dusting and rearranging displays.

Another new volunteer adventure came when we were asked to run a gift shop in the Danto facility across the street from Fleischman. We were able to find volunteers to open the shop, which lasted a few years, until Danto was sold, and we closed it.

At one point (dates leave me), I joined the board of Jewish Home for the Aged Auxiliary and found the meetings to be exciting. Getting together and getting to know each other was one more thing I felt I was part of, and a group of women who were long-time boardmembers would come up with great ideas for fundraising.

One idea was to "walk for ages." We had celebrities, such as Danny Raskin, and we had bagels, bottled water, and T-shirts. Many families came with their children and there were treats for the kids. I worked behind the counter, registering people, and handing out T-shirts.

Another idea was the wine tasting, which was held in the beautiful outdoor area behind the Fleischman Residence/Blumberg Plaza. The evening was perfect, with hors d'oeuvres to go with the wine. Many people came, including my family, and I was happy to introduce them to the other participants. Again, more people joined that night. Back then, we sent out mailings for all our events, and I helped get those mailings out.

The ideas were all successful. Many of our members joined at these events. Time has moved along, and I can remember the many years I was involved off and on with Jewish Senior Life.

I now volunteer at Sharon's boutique in the Fleischman Residence and love my job and the people I meet there.

I am 96, and I am a FRIEND of Jewish Senior Life.

Rose, 96, lives at Hechtman Apartments. She had a lifelong career in retail starting when she was 15 and working in a dress shop. She has three children, Janice (Larry) Cohen, Gary (Terri) Cooper, Jackie (Michael) Epstein; five grandchildren, Jordan, Aaron, Ben, Danny, and Sarah; and four great-grandchildren, Kai, Nora, Hanna, and Lucy. In addition to volunteering in the boutique, Rose plays mahjongg and Rummikub with a regular group.

MY BEST FRIENDS
AUDREY DEMAK

MY BEST FRIENDS

When I was very young, my father told me, "My kinde, if you can count friends on five fingers, you will be blessed." I have remembered that all my life.

Well, I am blessed. As a youngster, my besties were Ilene Libidinsky and Barbara Rosenthal in New York. After moving to Detroit in fourth grade, my bestie was Dolores Wisotsky — we were glued at the hip — and that endured until she married and I went off to nursing school. During that time, Morton, my fiancé, became my bestie.

One of my friends was a skating coach who I met years ago when my sons were playing hockey. Since I was at the hockey rink often, I took up skating and then ice dancing, which I loved. I even entered some competitions. The coach and I became good friends. However, I returned to work about 10 or 15 years ago, so I didn't have time to skate. After that, I gave it up because I was concerned about falling.

Now I live at Meer Apartments, where I reconnected with a high school acquaintance, Ester Dine, and we have become good friends. My other new bestie is Margaret Pathak, who is from India. When she moved into Meer, we took a liking to each other. She has had lots of interesting experiences — teaching in Mother Teresa's convent school in India, for example.

There are a lot of nice people and life options here at Meer if you want to take advantage of them. It's important to come out and make an effort. I am very fond of everyone in Meer's Creative Writing Class. I've learned what I want as a friend, and I consider myself to be a very loyal and real friend.

One of my best friends is Shelby, my very special pet dog who has been an important part of my life for three years. Shelby sometimes participates with me in Meer's Creative Writing Class. In one of her recent submissions, I am the mom:

> It's Sunday morning and while my mom has a few free minutes, I thought it would be a good time to say hi.

Life is good at Meer, and Mom is very involved in activities and is enjoying them.

Simba, my fiancé, comes by and visits when he can, and sometimes our friend Lynne takes us for a long walk around the whole property. I think she will be here today for that.

I really enjoy sitting out in the lobby sometimes in the evening and getting to meet more residents. Last week, I had a special surprise. Mom took me to her Creative Writing Class, and I got to meet with all the talented writers — so much fun.

So, you see, my father was right, and I am so blessed. Shelby and I understand how important social connections and friendship are. We reach out to our Meer neighbors and enjoy our time with them and with each other. We understand that real friends are hard to come by.

Audrey, 88, has lived at Meer Apartments for just over a year. Born in New York, Audrey came to Michigan at nine years old, graduated from Central High School, and completed the Harper Hospital Nursing School program in 1956. She worked as a nurse in the outpatient ophthalmology department at Sinai Hospital as well as in a medical/surgical unit. Her nursing experience was helpful while she cared for her late husband when he was ill for three years. She has three sons, Steven Demak, Ronald Demak, and Barry Demak, and two grandchildren, Nicholas and Samuel.

Audrey worked as a part-time private duty nurse until she moved to Meer. She believes in having a positive outlook and eagerly seeks opportunities to make new friends and explore various activities at Meer.

BITTER/SWEET
MARILYN DIZIK

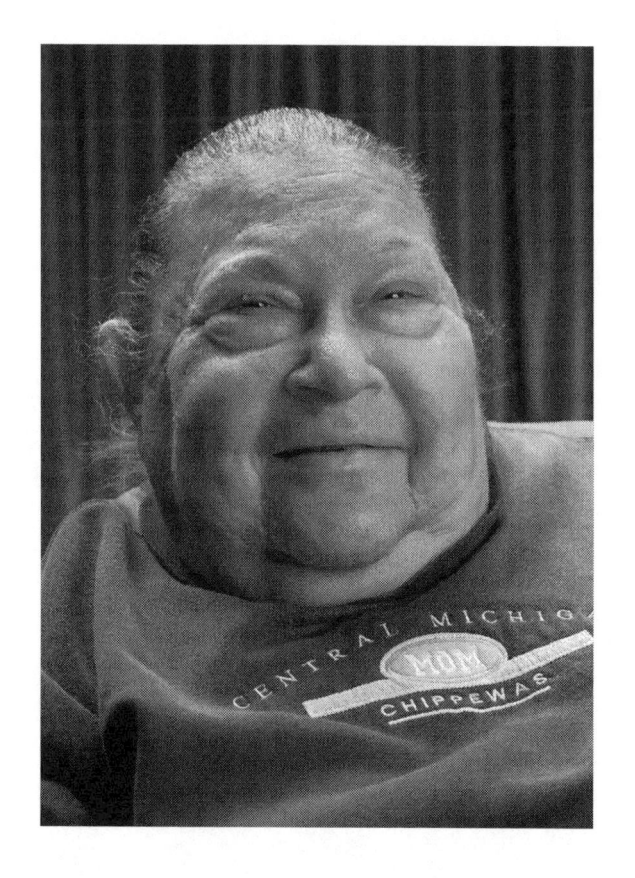

It was June 29th, a Friday. I had been down for breakfast and came back to my room because we didn't have anything planned until 11:00 am. There was a knock at the door. It was my younger brother, Eddie, and my sister-in-law, Rita. I had been here almost a month, and they said they had come to see where I was living.

Half an hour later, my son Jason came in. There were several knocks on the door and each time, Jason went out into the hallway while I sat in my chair. Finally, I said, "What's going on here? What's going on in the hall that I don't know anything about?" So, Jason came over and told me that my niece Emily had passed away. She was 24 years old.

Emily was my brother Bruce's younger daughter. At that time, my two brothers had been estranged for years and didn't speak to each other. But when Eddie and Rita found out Bruce had lost his daughter, Eddie called him and left a message saying how awful it was. The next day, Bruce called him back and asked if he and Rita would come to the funeral.

So, it took Emily's death to bring the two brothers together. They're not close, but at least they talk to each other.

Apparently, the night before she died, Emily hadn't felt well. She had juvenile rheumatoid arthritis. She was diagnosed as a teenager, and there wasn't a single day she wasn't in pain. Because of her juvenile rheumatoid arthritis, she had all kinds of health issues, including shingles when she was 21. It had been on her face, and since one of her cousins had married a dermatologist, he took one look at it and knew it was shingles. She also had a ruptured ovarian cyst. Her doctor put her on birth control pills, which was one treatment method, but one of its side effects was blood clots.

I always took my nieces out for their birthdays when they were little. We went to lunch and we went shopping, and I let them choose what they wanted, within reason. At seven years old, Emily wanted this fancy dollhouse for her birthday. I said,

"Sure," and we got the dollhouse. She was overjoyed and grateful. Emily was sunshine, and I was glad I could make her so happy.

The night before she died, her parents wanted to take her to the hospital but she said no, saying every time she went to the hospital, she was admitted for something or other. So, she lay down and her mother, Susan, lay down with her until she fell asleep. Susan got up at 5:00 am and checked in on Emily. Emily was sleeping, so Susan went back to bed. At about 7:00 am, she got up again and found that Emily had stopped breathing.

They called 911 and they sent the police and the paramedics. The first thing the police asked them was if she might have gotten into bad drugs, and of course, their answer was, "No, our daughter doesn't do drugs."

"How do you know?" the police asked in response. Bruce went to the cupboard, opened it, and showed them all the drugs Emily was on because of her juvenile rheumatoid arthritis. Bruce said, "These are all her drugs. She wouldn't take anything else."

But the police still questioned it.

By the time Bruce and Susan got to the hospital, Emily had been pronounced dead. The ER doc thought it was a pulmonary embolism, a blood clot possibly caused by the birth control pills. Then they were told that the police wanted an autopsy, and both Bruce and Susan said, "Absolutely not; we're Jewish, we don't do autopsies." Their doctor and their rabbi both said if the authorities wanted an autopsy, they had no choice.

"Why do you have to cut into my beautiful daughter?" asked Bruce. But they did an autopsy anyway. The funeral was scheduled for that Sunday morning. As far as I know, they never read the autopsy report.

The day Emily died was bittersweet for me. The staff thoughtfully ordered my lunch up to my room, but I hated being isolated with my grief and said I wanted to go downstairs. I wanted to be with people, so we went down. I was, of course, not my usual self at all.

That afternoon, Eddie, Rita, Jason, and his wife Emily came. We went into the chapel and they sat me down. Emily looked at me and said, "I'm pregnant." I was ecstatic that there was a new life coming into existence. They hadn't planned to tell me then; they had planned to wait a bit longer, but after they discussed it, and knowing how much I wanted a grandchild, they decided that I needed to know. That was the sweet part.

Eddie and Rita picked me up for the funeral. They had their daughter Vicki with them, and we met Jason and Emily at Kaufman's for the service, but we did not go to the cemetery. First of all, there was not going to be an easy way for me to maneuver with my walker, and secondly, Emily was pregnant, so I wouldn't let her go. Pregnant women don't go to the cemetery in Jewish tradition.

Eddie and Rita went to the cemetery and Jason and I dropped off Vicki and Emily at home, then went to Bruce and Susan's house to wait for them.

Later that afternoon, Jason told Bruce why Emily didn't go to the cemetery. Bruce came over and whispered, "Congratulations, Grandma," in my ear.

Marilyn, 76, lives in Fleischman Residence/Blumberg Plaza. A native Detroiter, she has a son, Jason Dizik, and a grandson, Evan. A Certified Business Continuity Professional, Marilyn has worked with computers since 1971, programming and designing applications and serving as the head of disaster recovery for computer systems. She has also worked in HR systems, producing payroll checks and reporting.

Marilyn has a profound interest in Judaism and graduated from the United Hebrew School Leadership Teacher Training Institute as well as from the Florence Melton Adult School of Judaism. She taught first grade Sunday school at Temple Beth El for 18 years. Marilyn likes to read, draw, paint, do crossword puzzles, and spend time with her grandson, Evan.

THE SOUNDS AROUND ME
HARRY DOREN

I am 90 years old now, living in a senior home, but I am no longer living alone.

I was born hearing-impaired, but not alone. I was a twin. My sister Beth was born with me but did not live long enough to grow up with me.

My memories of growing up are unclear, because I could not hear what was happening around me. I was difficult to live with due to my anger about not having the communications skills to talk and listen to my parents and older brothers. Two of my brothers were healthy, but the third brother died from spinal meningitis. My mother was never the same.

My anger and frustration caused me to become destructive. I broke the large kitchen window one morning when I couldn't find my mother. She had gone grocery shopping and I didn't know.

I did not do well in public school due to poor hearing. The teacher told my mother to send me to a school for the deaf on the east side of Detroit. It took an hour and a half to get there by streetcar. My mother told the streetcar conductor to drop me off on Stanton Street. I did not want to go alone, but my mother forced me.

I learned to read lips and wore headphones in class to amplify the sound. My spoken language improved.

During my teenage years, one of my brothers bought me a pair of hearing aids. I improved in everyday spoken language, and it helped in my home communications. I loved being able to listen to the radio with the hearing aids; before that, I had to increase the radio volume and press my ear to the radio to hear my favorite show, *Inner Sanctum*.

During my years at the school for the deaf, I was able to learn American Sign Language and to communicate with my fellow students. Plus, I began to prepare for the hearing world. I learned to speak with the teacher without using sign language.

There were times I did not want to wear hearing aids. People stared at the aids in my ears, and I wanted to look normal. But a good friend invited me to join him to go to a dude ranch up north in Brevort, Michigan. The only way I could go with him was if I wore my hearing aids. We went, and I learned to ride a horse.

He was a young, untrained horse. He began to run fast on the trail, and I was unable to slow him down. But I steered him into a densely wooded area where he couldn't run.

He slowed and then began to walk, and I jumped off. Then, he lowered his head and lay down, trapping my legs against his body. The camp guide came and got the horse up on his four legs. I told the guide I was going to walk back to camp, but he told me to get back on the horse or I would never want to ride a horse again.

I have to admit that my horse-riding experience made me aware of the sounds of nature, of birds singing and the horse running on the trail. The sounds through my hearing aids made me aware of my environment.

From that day, my everyday hearing has helped me be aware of life around me. I began to accept my hearing loss, becoming aware of everyday sounds and not being concerned about people looking at my hearing aids — all thanks to my good friend.

He made me accept my deafness and made me a better man. Now, I'm not afraid to jump into anything. As I get older, I am still that man, and I still have that wonderful friend. I recently drove three hours to tell him thank you for his support face to face.

Harry, 90, lives at Hechtman Apartments. He has a master's in vocational rehab services and spent his career serving the hearing-impaired and deaf populations. Harry enjoys socializing with his Hechtman neighbors, especially catching up with people from "the old neighborhood."

TICK TOCK
TONI FONTANA

TICK TOCK

"Yea, though I walk through the valley of the shadow of death, I shall fear no evil."

Dying isn't the part that concerns me. I'm not in a race to see who will live the longest.

After the deaths of my husband, my sister (who was my best friend), my youngest son, my mother, my father, and many more, I'm already one of the last runners-up in my circle.

I remember when I was 13 and I was asked how long I wanted to live, I said I didn't want to live past 35. In my mind, I thought 35 was very old, and I didn't want to get old. When I turned 35, I felt I was living my best life while family and friends said with the way I was living and the friends I kept, I might not make it to 40. They said I was living life too fast and taking too many risks, like every day was my last.

So, now I am over 60 years young, still waking up every morning. They say growing old is graceful, but I don't see much that is graceful in getting old, with all its aches and pains and fear of disease.

Tick, tock, tick, tock...

Three years ago, I moved into a new apartment complex for seniors.

I looked back at all the lovers I had and all the loves I'd lost. I thought the last one was the last forever. In thinking that I would be alone for the duration, it seems I was wrong again.

Well, surprisingly, I woke up again, but this morning was different. The sun was shining extra brightly while the summer breezes were perfectly soft against my skin. I could hear the birds singing so melodically I could have sworn they were angels singing praises to the Lord. But of course, I had to be letting my imagination run away with me.

While taking a short walk, I was looking at how the grass and the trees were always praising G-d, reaching and waving as they gave G-d the glory. After my walk, I returned to my building only to finish my outing by sitting on the front bench, making small talk with my neighbors. Later, I decided to make it an early evening.

This lovely day was winding down, and I had enjoyed it so much that I felt like it couldn't get any better and it was time to call it a night. As I entered the building and approached the elevator, I pushed the button to bring the elevator down to the first floor. I heard that distinct sound of the elevator bell ringing to let me know it had arrived. As the doors opened and I was about to enter, I looked in and, lo and behold, I gazed upon the most beautiful man I have ever seen.

There was a smile in his eyes that was directed right at me. I was so mesmerized. I knew he was speaking, but I couldn't comprehend what he was saying. He had the most beautiful blue eyes and dark wavy hair. He had a soft olive complexion with a radiant glow around him. I allowed my eyes to look at him from head to toe. As the door began to close, I suddenly began to understand what he was saying. He had asked for my name, and I told him it was Toni with an "i". Awkwardly, I asked him for his name, and he said it was Joshua. He asked if he could call me sometime and I said, "Yes," and gave him my number.

The next day at about noon, my phone rang and I answered with anticipation. Yes, it was Joshua, and as he spoke to me in a deep calming voice, saying, "This is Joshua, Is this Toni?" I said, "Yes," and the last romance of my life began.

Tick, tock, tick, tock...

We made a little small talk and he asked if he could come by to visit soon. I said, "Yes," and we set a time for 7:00 pm that evening. As I began reconsidering my carefully chosen outfit, the time had almost arrived, and I was waiting excitedly. Suddenly, there was a knock at the door. I ran to look in the mirror and check my face to make sure I looked presentable. *What will be will be*, I decided and opened the door.

When I opened the door and looked at Joshua, I suddenly realized how tall and handsome he really was. Before I recovered enough to invite him to sit down or offer him a beverage, I was distracted by his glowing aura and pulled into his mysterious eyes.

He began to tell me all the deep mysteries of the world. He showed me how man was created and why. We travelled through the galaxies as he held my hand, and he explained how the stars were hung in space and how the sun and moon had a distinct relationship. He explained how and why the animals and all creatures were put on all the planets. I was overwhelmed by all the beauty and knowledge that had been put into creating the circle of life.

I can only imagine how this all sounds, but it was so much more than I can find words to describe. After these wonderful journeys, I asked Joshua how he knew all this and how we were able to travel through space and time. Finally, he responded:

"I've been waiting for you to ask me that. Most of my brides don't take in as much knowledge as you have before wanting to know who I really am. Well, I am the *I AM*. I am the Father, the Son, and the Holy Spirit. I am Jesus, or Joshua. I am the Alpha and the Omega, the Beginning and the End. I am the One Love that you will never lose. While you are waiting for our wedding ceremony, I will be preparing a place for us, and in the meantime, I will always be with you. I will never leave you or forsake you."

My heart has been so full and happy since that day. Now, He continues to walk with me and talk with me and tell me how much He loves me. I have had a change of heart about growing old gracefully. Growing old is graceful now that I know the wedding of a lifetime is waiting for me, to the King of Kings and the Lord of Lords.

I have a few words of wisdom for you all. When your King comes knocking at your door, please answer before it is too late to live and grow old in the grace of the Lord — because the clock is ticking!

Toni Curtis Fontana was born February 20, 1953, in Detroit. She was the sixth of eight children in a family that included four girls and four boys. Toni attended the public Mackenzie schools as well as the Catholic St. Catherine's and St. Cecelia high schools in Detroit. After graduating, Toni became the first woman to work for the Detroit Board of Education Building and Trade as a construction laborer. She also worked on the People Mover in downtown Detroit.

Additionally, Toni became certified as a missionary and evangelist at Solomon's Temple Church of the Church of our Lord Jesus Christ (COOLJC) and organized the Self-Esteem Regimen for at-risk and inner-city children. The author of several books of poetry inspired by the Holy Spirit, Toni is the mother of four children and eight grandchildren. She says she never plans to retire "from the work [she is] called on to do."

FINDING CONTENTMENT
SHMUEL GRAYBAR

SHMUEL GRAYBAR

I am 67 years old. I was born in California, grew up in Detroit, and lived most of my life in Crown Heights, Brooklyn, New York. My Jewish religion and community are the most important things for me.

I was brought up "sorta Conservative," but was drawn to Orthodoxy starting around the age of 12. I had my bar mitzvah in an Orthodox shul. I was attracted to the religious pride and positivity of Chabad-Lubavitch around the time I was in college.

I had a difficult childhood, but my Judaism has helped me see my internal and external challenges in a more positive light. Both the Torah and life experience have taught me to let go of my need to control everything, go more with the flow, and have faith in G-d to run things.

This is not to say that everything has always gone the way I liked, but even when things went sour, something good and profitable came out of it. For example, although my marriage didn't work out, it did produce a daughter who is beautiful inside and out. She lives in Crown Heights with her new husband, who loves her like a queen.

I also take pride in the many creative things I've done. I have illustrated six books for children, done political cartoons for a couple of newspapers, painted murals for different public places, and taught both religious and secular subjects in schools.

I came to Prentis in 2018, and my time here has been very pleasant. I have made some good friends and enjoyed the dedicated care of the Jewish Senior Life staff. I pray they are able to continue being a source of warmth and goodness for our community for many years to come.

Shmuel, 67, lives at Prentis Apartments. He has one daughter, Bracha Tova. Shmuel is a graphic designer and a teacher. He teaches Judaism and helps people get closer to G-d.

A NIGHT AT THE CATSKILLS
HARRIET HESSENTHALER

Throughout my life, I have always been interested in the theatre. As a child, my friends, cousins, and I would make up plays to sing and dance in. My uncle would take us all to family dinners to perform for all our relatives.

Once I married and had children, my sons enjoyed seeing their mother dress up as an "eccentric" grandmother from Mars. Later, my grandchildren loved visiting Bubbie Harriett's home, because together we would make costumes with wigs, scarves, and clothes for our family plays.

A few years ago, I learned about a great aunt, Vera Gordon, who performed in more than 50 silent and talking movies. Maybe I caught the theatre bug from her.

While my children were going to school, I also continued my education and graduated with a degree as a recreational therapist. My internship was at Southfield Senior Center helping two seniors, Rose and Evelyn, start a theatre group. They wanted help producing a senior center show.

We decided on a variety show of singers, dancers, comedians, and other talented performers, and we called it *A Night at the Catskills*. After advertising in the senior center paper, we were pleasantly surprised at the big response.

After rehearsing for a month, it was very gratifying to see how important this play was to Rose and Evelyn. It gave their lives meaning. At the same time, I learned that it was not how many years you lived, but your willingness to live life to the fullest.

A Night at the Catskills was extremely successful, and more than 100 seniors attended. Everyone thanked us for our hard work and wanted me to produce another play. I have never forgotten the joy I received from working with that wonderful group of people.

The experience gave me the confidence to continue to produce more shows with other senior groups. The shows gave people something to do — interact with others — and brought some meaning to their lives.

Today, I continue to use these skills at Hechtman Apartments, where I founded a Reader's Theatre. We recently had our inaugural production. The readers are Hechtman residents who choose the skits they want to perform. We rehearsed our recent production for five months and became a close group. Seeing our camaraderie has encouraged others to participate in our next production. This activity has brought joy and humor into all our lives along with the satisfaction that we brought to our audience.

I have also greatly benefitted. The fun and sense of purpose this activity provides is priceless. I hope to continue this program for many years ahead.

Harriet, 84, was born in Detroit. She graduated from Madonna University at age 52, with a degree in gerontology and recreational therapy, and then worked in senior centers as a recreational therapist. She loves music and theater, especially Fiddler on the Roof *and Andrea Bocelli. She also loves traveling and photography. Harriet's children and grandchildren are the joy of her life. Her children are Mark (Djabriz), Bruce (Susan), Darren (of blessed memory), and Lori, and her four grandchildren are Gabe, Emily, Noah, and Nitro.*

BETTER PLANS
BONNIE HUBERT, CNA, HHA

Before moving into Hechtman Apartments, I worked as a certified nursing assistant, specializing in geriatrics and giving one-on-one home healthcare to the elderly. Eventually, I came to realize the importance of community life and its benefits. It was something I was unable to provide for my home healthcare clients.

I've worked in a lot of facilities, and I have worked privately with a lot of seniors. I wrote the following poem when I was working with them. Hechtman has saved me from a lot of the issues I mention in the poem; I took my own advice and made better plans.

Senior Lament

We are old and we're cranky, can't live on our own.
When the staff doesn't like us, we're left all alone.

Our aches and our pains are getting us down.
And when we need help, there's no one around.

They put us in homes and quickly shut the door.
Frankly, our kids just don't care anymore.

We lost our freedom; our independence is gone.
We're depressed and lonely, so we sleep all day long.

Everyone's in a hurry. They think it's a joke.
But they won't think it's funny when they're in the same boat.

They must learn to slow down and stop running in circles.
Start facing the fact that this is no dress rehearsal.

Soon they will be in our place, with no one to care.
Finding out we need help just to walk up the stairs.

We might find an aide with compassion and respect.
But our family complains when they write them their check.

Can't see, can't hear, and can't live all alone.
They solve all our problems with nursing homes.

They are frightened and confused. The burden is great.
Making all our decisions and having no time to wait.

We were too busy and should have made better plans.
Now, it's our fault; we're in our children's hands.

Out of guilt, our kids visit, then bid us good day.
Make up excuses; they don't want to stay.

Life looks dark and gloomy, with no hope in sight.
Only you can make changes and fight for our rights.

I have thought all about it; you must change the event.
So that you don't get lost in the "Senior Lament."

I've been living at Hechtman for 11 years. I was 65 when I moved in, and now I am 76.

In my opinion, people don't move into senior living facilities soon enough. Living here takes all the stress off, and I think people would be happier if they figured that out sooner. The first apartment I saw here, I was happy with. I said I would take it, and I've been there ever since.

I wrote the poem "Senior Lament" while I was still working, having observed many of the issues that seniors have to deal with and having heard them express their frustrations. So, I took my own advice to avoid those problems and moved into the Hechtman community. And I love it here. There are activities to do all the time. I'm not just sitting around in my house with nothing to do.

Bonnie Hubert, 76, lives at Hechtman Apartments. She is a lifelong Detroit resident and has one son, Ben Hubert. Bonnie worked as a certified nursing assistant specializing in geriatrics and even in retirement still likes to take care of people. She studied retail marketing and, at age 19, had a boutique called The Great Escape on Woodward Avenue.

Bonnie also taught fiber art and weaving classes and wrote a book on it. She keeps busy managing Tuesday Night Bingo and selling 50/50 raffle tickets each month, playing Rummikub daily, and shopping at Sharon's Boutique from time to time.

MY TWO PASSIONS
ELEANOR JOHNSON

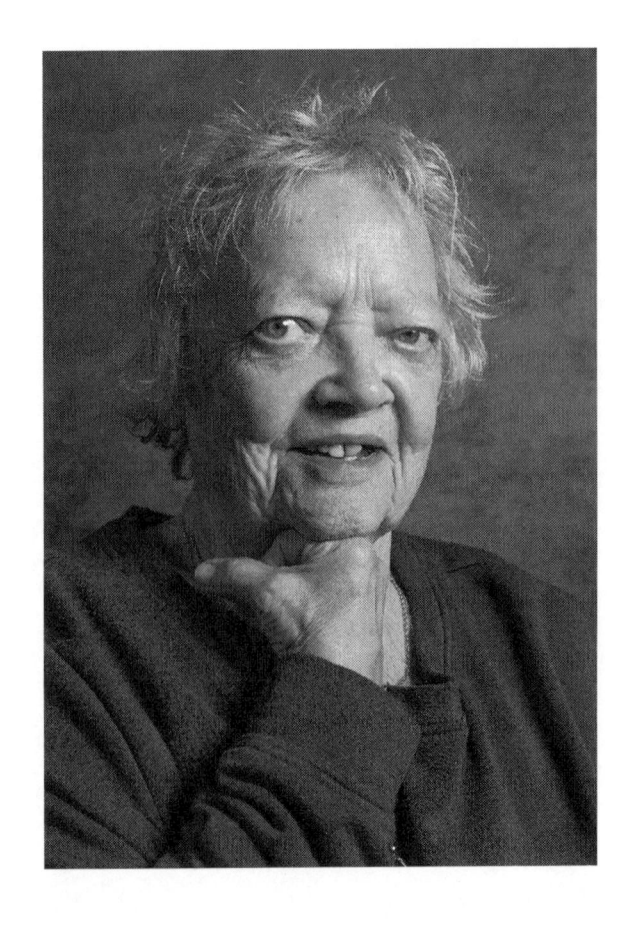

I have been a seamstress most of my life, making my own clothes, including my wedding dress, and clothes for my four daughters. So, when my church signed up to help the victims of the hurricane in Haiti, I saw an opportunity to put my sewing skills to work for an important cause.

I started making dresses for women and girls — every style dress you can think of in all different sizes. I made dresses for everyone from babies to adult women. Then, I decided I should make clothes for boys, so I found cotton fabric to make shorts because it's hot in Haiti. All in all, I've made thousands of clothing items to send to Haiti.

When COVID-19 came, I switched to making masks. I just kept making them and putting them in a basket outside my front door so people could come and take what they needed. This was before you could buy them.

Then, my daughter in New York told me she had heard that Native Americans out West needed masks, because the men have bigger faces than available masks could cover. So, I started making masks for them. Later, I happened to be at Dr. Stern's, my foot doctor. I had a mask with me, so I showed it to him and told him what I was doing. He told me not to send them myself but to bring them to his office and he would send them out. Dr. Stern used his own account to send masks to different states and countries where he knew masks were needed. It has given me great joy to do this important work.

Another thing I do that brings me great joy is cooking. I will find a recipe, make it, and then take it down to the café for people to taste. I encourage them to take one little bite and give me their review. This summer they have been calling me the salad and soup queen, since I have been making southern cornbread salad and gazpacho. One of my specialties is carrot cake. I make them and give them out to residents here, and I make other cakes and dishes for picnics. I make everything from scratch and people are always asking me for recipes.

So, I found my purpose and my passions in these later years by making clothes for people in need and sharing my love of food through my cooking.

Eleanor, 82, lives at Prentis Apartments. She was born in Georgia but spent much of her life in Madison Heights and Hazel Park. She has four daughters, Lori Johnson/Golden, Kelly Horvath, and Tina Jognson/Burgers; nine grandchildren, Jason, Sunni, Chelsea, Harrison, Cullen, Addie, Paige, Tyler, and Jasper; and nine great-grandchildren, Cade, Lee, Gavin, Kaesyn, Clark, Eliza, Harrison Jr., Malkom, and Marrya. Eleanor is currently fostering a cat and writing her life story.

THE FAMILY MAN
BERNIE JONAS

I am a family man. The proof is on the walls of my Meer Apartment living room, which is covered with photographs. My two sons and my late daughter provided me with 108 offspring — grandchildren, great-grandchildren, and great-great-grandchildren.

I started out keeping track of all of them, but then I lost count. Now, I just keep track of the number; the people in these pictures are some of my rewards.

I never had a Jewish education except for bar mitzvah, but Judaism was very important to me and my late wife Pauline, who came from an observant family. We were married for 62 years and decided early to send our children to Yeshivath Beth Yehudah. I am proud to say that I have one son and three grandsons who are Orthodox rabbis. I didn't care if my children were religious, but I wanted them to know what it meant to be good Jews.

I was the oldest of six boys and six girls, and my own Jewish education was enhanced by my father. Several rabbis once visited my father's Eastside Detroit grocery store seeking donations. My father told them to return later when his oldest sons were there. We talked to them about their charities, and then my father told us to go upstairs and write them a check.

Pauline and I were married at Congregation B'nai Moshe on Dexter in Detroit and were on-and-off members for decades. I still attend B'nai Moshe every Shabbat, with the help of my fellow congregant Rita Kaplan. Rita drives me, my sister Lillian Fox (who lives in the adjacent apartment), and Meer resident Edith Maniker to and from the weekly services.

I've lived at Meer since early 2022, and I like living there because it's mostly all Jews. It's all kosher food, and there are lots of programs. My only disappointment is that more of the residents don't attend the programming.

My biggest pleasure is when my family and friends call me. One of my grandsons calls me every day. Others are sure to keep my telephone busy on Fridays when I get regular calls wishing me a "good Shabbes."

I also have a friend I met five years after Pauline passed, Esther Morger. I talk to Esther twice a day, every day. I was one of the people who urged her a year ago to move away from Detroit to be closer to family, but obviously we are still very good friends.

To celebrate my 100th birthday in August, a grandson in California planned a kosher celebration at a restaurant near Meer. It had to be kosher, and it was, of course, a little expensive. People came from New York, New Jersey, Massachusetts, California, and Texas. I was hoping to see my sister who lives in Israel, but that's a hard trip.

Family means everything to me. I still tear up when people ask about Pauline, my parents, or my late daughter. We are family. It's what I tell all of them when we call or write — we are family!

Bernie, 100, lives at Meer Apartments. He was the purchasing and traffic manager for three nut and bolt suppliers, winning an award as National Fastening Industry Man of the Year. He volunteered at Yad Ezra kosher food bank for 20 years and was honored as Yad Ezra Man of the Year. He was also an 8 Over 80 Tikkun Olam Award honoree. Bernie's children are Mark Jonas, Rabbi Shmaya Jonas, and the late Suzanne Winkleman (of blessed memory). He has 108 grandchildren, great-grandchildren, and great-great-grandchildren. Eight of his grandchildren are named in loving memory of his late wife, Pauline (of blessed memory).

CANCER IS A PAIN IN THE BUTT!
NANCY KALEF

My name is Nancy Kalef. I've lived a charmed life. I'm married to a wonderful man, Manny (Maynard) Kalef. We both are in second marriages, ours for 44+ years. It has had its ups and downs, but we have lived happily in a very pretty condo for 37 of the 44 years.

I've been a leader most of my life. After graduation from Mackenzie High School in Detroit in 1951, I took one year of college, got married at 18, had a beautiful daughter at 20, and lived in Huntsville, Alabama, for seven years.

Upon returning to Detroit, I started my work career, spending over 50 years in offices, mostly in management positions. My last gig was my own business, Let's Get Organized, from 1998 to 2001. I went to homes and offices to organize closets, cupboards, and paperwork. My business card tag line read: *"Better Than Your Mother!"* It turned out to be my favorite work of my whole career. Making a difference in others' lives fulfilled me.

In 1980, we moved into Lincoln Shire Towne Homes Condominiums in Southfield, and I was tapped almost immediately to be secretary of the homeowners association. A few years later, I took on the presidency of the association, and that lasted until 2016. We were a self-managed association, and I was called on nearly daily to manage the exterior of the property as well as oversee work that residents needed done inside their units. I was the go-to person for contractors, service providers, handymen, landscapers, roadway repairs, and on and on *ad nauseam*!

One morning, after a resident called me for something he needed, I hung up the phone and said to my husband, "That's it! I cannot do this job anymore. It's time to move to Meer Apartments."

Truth be told, we had already looked at several options. One potential move was out of the question financially, and another was too non-Jewish. Even though we are not extremely religious, I could not think of living in a facility that had non-kosher food.

My immediate action was to call Jewish Senior Life and speak to Tracey Proghovnick, leasing agent and daughter of dear friends of ours. The rest is magical history.

We had an appointment with Leslie Richardson, the building's social worker. She showed us several apartments, including one that hadn't been cleaned yet after the former tenants moved. Not only was it absolutely perfect for what we needed, but the dents in the carpet showed exactly where we would put our furniture. We thought that was a good omen!

We signed on the dotted line almost immediately and prepared our apartment to become our "forever home." We created a smaller version of our condo and moved in.

We had only lived here a short time when I started getting involved. The building and grounds became our home. If there was something I felt didn't portray Meer in the best way, I spoke up. When we had resident council meetings, I watched the executive board handle their duties. When residents were unhappy about something, I took it upon myself to check out the complaint.

At the next council election, I was elected secretary. Two years later, I was elected president of the resident council, and I have held that position since 2019.

Now, in November 2023, I'm turning 90! Imagine 90 years of living and what we oldsters have seen in our lives; so many changes, so much to adjust to.

Two months ago, I was diagnosed with cancer of the anus — not a subject many are willing to discuss, but as I tell everyone I speak with, everyone has an anus and everyone pees and poops! Oprah Winfrey desensitized me many years ago when she used to talk about pee and poop.

I thought I had hemorrhoids for a couple of years. Until I started to bleed, I didn't pay much attention; I didn't bother them, and they didn't bother me. Then I decided to go to a physician who does the banding technique. I thought it would be a 15-minute procedure, but the doctor wanted to see more.

The gastroenterologist did a sigmoidoscope. Suspicious tissues were biopsied and lab tests proved squamous cell carcinoma. By that time, I was not shocked.

Then came many more tests: CT scans, blood tests, a PET scan. More blood tests showed more anemia — no wonder I was always running out of steam.

Then, treatment started with Dr. Kenneth Levin in radiology and Dr. Maria Diab in oncology of Henry Ford Hospital. Both are amazing, brilliant, and the kindest two human beings in the world.

Bottom line: Cancer of the anus, cure rate 98%.

Treatment entailed two rounds of chemo, each 24 hours a day for five days straight. I also had 30+ radiation treatments and am taking advantage of healing touch therapy and acupuncture. My best purchase for healing was a bidet!

By the time this is published, I expect to be 100% cured and "living the good life" with my wonderful husband and neighbors at Meer Apartments.

Nancy Kalef, 90, lives at the Meer Apartments with her husband Manny. Between the two of them, they have two children, Judy (Paul) Lipson and Ellen (Lou) Feldman; six grandchildren, Brian, Rachel, Stacey, Michael, Jeremy, and Abby; and eight great-grandchildren, Jack, Kayla, Stella, Marielle, Max, Henry, Zara, and Jake.

Nancy worked as an office manager before starting her organizing business, Let's Get Organized. She still likes to organize and is president of the Meer Resident Council. She also enjoys making beaded jewelry, writing, and spending time with friends and family.

THE YELLOW BOX
RUTH KATZ

I thought it would look so pretty on the shelf, and I wanted something to remember our late 1970s travels in Florence, Italy. The stitching was beautiful, and the color so different than what I otherwise saw. It looked like a little treasure chest among all the *tchotchkes* for sale. My late husband, Herbie, and I were fortunate to travel the world since we co-owned a travel agency. I had no idea such a small, delicate item would hold such a big meaning and span decades, connecting generations.

My grandkids, now grown and most with their own children, and now my great-grandchildren, call it and will forever know it as "the Yellow Box."

As mentioned, it started as just a pretty piece for my shelves. Once my children had our grandchildren — one born every year from 1982 through 1986, Monica, Ariel, Nicole, and Michele — and they became old enough, I noticed that they always wanted to hold and open the Yellow Box. And of course, they started fighting over it.

I had to think of something. How could I involve all four of my grandchildren, but be fair about the Yellow Box? I remembered it came with a little key, and well, kids love games. That sparked their favorite game out of all the toys and games we ever bought: I would hide the key, and whoever found it would get to open the box. I never hid the key *in* anything; it was only ever in plain sight or on something eye-level in full view. In the box, there would always be something inside for all four grandchildren — what a win-win!

Of course, the prizes changed over the years. At first, I put candy and little toys in the Yellow Box; then it became gift certificates, and then, of course, cash as they got older. I loved seeing the pure joy on their faces as they got to open it. I loved watching and hearing them giggle as they looked for the key. I loved knowing that these memories I was gaining were also memories they were making.

As the years went on, I started running out of places to hide the key. As my grandchildren got older, they started getting smarter, asking me what floor and/or what room the key was in. Once, I even hid it outside; they looked so confused, and it was so much fun for all. Their excitement was everything to me.

It was a little box, but with huge meaning. It became the most fun and greatest tradition for our family.

Now, I get to hide the key for a new generation — for my six great-grandchildren, four of whom are local. I get to experience this amazing tradition now with Sadie, Libby, Sonny, and Nomi, and, when they come into town, Emma and Evan. What an honor that I get to do it all over again. Sadie says it's her absolute favorite thing and races to the box after saying hello to me when she comes over.

"Nanny, can we look for the key now?" she and her younger sister Libby eagerly ask after they race through the door, bouncing with excitement. Just like my grandchildren before them, they know the key will be hidden if they come over.

It's such a unique and important tradition that brings happiness, love, and joy. I will pass down the Yellow Box one day and can only hope it continues for many generations. The box's yellow color has faded a bit, but the significance and purpose have not. Seeing the kids' faces is priceless, no matter how much I've spent filling the box for over 35 years (and counting).

That is the real *key* to this.

Ruth, 91, lives at Meer Apartments. She was born and raised in Detroit and co-founded a travel agency with her late husband, Herbie. Together, they traveled the world. She has a daughter, Debbie Holtz; a son, the late Steve Katz (of blessed memory); four grandchildren, Monica, Ari, Nicole, and Michele; and six great-grandchildren, Sadie, Libby, Sonny, Emma, Nomi, and Evan. When she isn't volunteering at the Meer Boutique for JSL, you can find Ruth doing crossword puzzles. Ruth loves sewing. She was an avid ice skater, and still loves to watch skating on TV.

FREEDOM
HARRIET KOVACS

This whole episode started at Shaarey Zedek. I was at an event, and suddenly I couldn't walk. I left in a wheelchair and went home. I made it to the bathroom, but then I just couldn't move.

We had to call the EMS to get me out. The stretcher wouldn't go into the bathroom. They helped me out of the bathroom and into the bedroom where there was more room, and then I was taken to Henry Ford Hospital. I never got a true diagnosis, other than incontinence. My body just went south. I was only there overnight, and then after that, they asked me which rehab I wanted to go to. I said I didn't care, which was a big mistake. I really didn't like it at the one they picked.

They weren't very nice. For one thing, I was in a diaper, and I needed to get changed because I was wetting all the time. When I called one of the people who was assigned to help me, she said, "I was just in your room two hours ago. I can't come back now." I was limited to how many times I was going to urinate. So that really disturbed me. I thought I really should have reported something like that, but I didn't. It was like my life was being ruled from the outside, and I didn't have my opinions heard. I was supposed to move to Fleischman, but I got COVID-19, so I had to wait there until I was over it.

I had a really nice aide at the rehab, but I had to get put to sleep at 10:00 pm, and I didn't want to go to bed that early. I could have stayed up, but then no one would come in 'til around midnight. I was very controlled with things like that. I was going to bed at 10:00 pm. I couldn't get up. I couldn't move my legs to get up when I was on the floor.

Then I came to Fleischman, and I liked having more freedom here. I could move. Sometimes I'm impatient, because I call for an aide and they don't come for a little while, but I've adjusted, and I understand they have other people with needs, too. Here, I can go outside. I can go where I want, and I don't have to tell anyone. There is more freedom.

There are also all kinds of activities. Maybe I feel more comfortable because most of the people are Jewish, so it's more like home.

In old age, basically everybody wants to plan your life. You have very little say in what you want.

I've been going to physical therapy, but I missed one week while my therapist was on vacation. I noticed the difference. I really need the physical therapy, and I wish I could have it three times a week for my lifetime, but good old Medicare won't let you do that. Yeah, that's kind of a problem — like you feel there are many more services and treatments you could access — but I did get an extra month, and I was surprised and relieved.

My husband Mike and I, we're funny because we bicker all the time. We're at different ends of the spectrum — politically and everything else — but, you know, we're happy with each other. But I fight with him all the time, and maybe I expect too much.

I was able to leave Fleischman for a visit home a few times, and as I walked into my house, I was disappointed to see that it was filthy. I told Mike I could understand things were not in place, but being dirty is another thing. That bothered me. My son said that I wasn't being very fair; Mike had just had surgery and all, and he couldn't go upstairs for the computer, so everything, every room, was really cluttered downstairs.

I've got a lot of faults too. I'm not saying I'm perfect at all, and I'm a nitpicker. What can I say? He does all the cooking and everything, and I'm appreciative, but I don't always show that I'm appreciative. That's what my son tells me.

After I leave Fleischman, I'll be home for a few months and then we're going to our home in Florida. I used to enjoy the pool, but now that freedom has been taken away from me because my big concern is urinating in the pool — I wouldn't want to take a chance. I should have a bed in the bathroom. I live in the bathroom.

I used to use a cane, but I was falling all the time, so I needed a walker. That's another restriction.

You know, over the course of this illness, it's like, "I can't do this, now I can't do that." You know, it goes with age.

But I still have that spirit of "I'm going to pick stuff up off the floor," even though I might fall down.

I recently gave up driving. I was in a traffic circle and put my foot on the gas when I shouldn't have and hit the curb and ruined two tires. I may have been on medication that prohibits driving while taking it.

Michael is good. He never says, "Look, you did this and you did that," and he doesn't make a point of saying, "What the heck did you do?" He just fixes what's broken. He's a good guy like that and does all the cooking and everything, and now, of course, he does all the driving too. But I don't want to just sit all the time. I want to be able to still move around and resume my mahjongg and Scrabble and stuff like that.

So, let me try to think of something that's good. I enjoy my grandchildren, and that came with age. I didn't have grandchildren before. I am home now, and I'm more appreciative, and things have continued to get better largely because Mike took me to a pain management doctor. My husband does everything he can to please me. He's a very loving person. My son does what he can to make me happy. My son and daughter-in-law and my daughter and son-in-law are always very helpful. I have wonderful friends who come to my house every week to play mahjongg.

There are a lot of senior activities that I can still do. I haven't done them for a while, but I did before. Maybe there are some senior trips or something. So long as there's a bathroom!

Harriet, 78, is a former resident of Fleischman Residence/Blumberg Plaza. She worked as a Welcome Wagon hostess and a preschool teaching assistant as well as owning a daycare. She has two children, Lisa Ginsburg and Larry Kovacs, and three grandchildren, Shelby, Nolan, and Camryn.

Harriet loves playing mahjongg and Scrabble, watching Tigers baseball and movies, volunteering, doing word games, and shopping. She loved to dance when she was younger and still likes to move to music. After leaving Fleischman, Harriet has returned regularly to volunteer.

NOTES FROM MY LIFE
HARRY KRIM

I worked at Ford Motor Company before the United States got into World War II. I worked as an inspector of engines for the B-26 bomber at Ford's Willow Run plant.

My father, Leon, came here in the early 1900s. He brought his family over from Europe. He owned the Riverside Hotel in Mt. Clemens, where I was born. My mother went to Austria to visit her mother just before the US got into World War II. She took my older siblings with her, and they wound up being stuck there for four years.

I was in a kids' rodeo when I was in Arizona in the 1930s. I had gone there to a camp because I had sinus problems — but then some kid squirted water up my nose from a drinking fountain and I had sinus problems again.

My wife Barbara died on our honeymoon. She had taken over driving the car from me while on our way to California. It happened in Ohio. The car swerved and we hit a boulder. I never got married again and that was my big mistake. I should have.

I attended Central High School in Detroit and lettered in track. I ran in the county-wide marathon with hundreds and hundreds of runners and came in 40th.

I was also a boxer and went to the Golden Gloves semi-finals. I was in the lightweight division. I was 135 pounds then and I wish I was that now. I'm probably 155 now, down from 167, and I'm still trying to lose weight. When my photo is taken, I always turn a little bit to the left because my nose was broken when I was boxing.

Like a lot of Detroiters, I saw Barbra Streisand at the Caucus Club. I'd go there once a week and get a fillet steak. I once saw the Shah of Iran while I was skiing in Aspen, and I once had lunch with actor Robert Stack in Los Angeles. We were sitting at adjacent tables in a restaurant and got to talking. He had just played the role of a bullfighter in a movie.

Before penicillin, my father had strep throat and died. I

caught strep, but had no problem. My sister had strep and it affected her kidneys. She died from it nine years later.

My brothers owned several movie theaters, the Bijou and the Park in Detroit and the Macomb in Mt. Clemens. Sometimes I operated the movie projectors and sometimes I would be the movie theater master of ceremonies. We would hand out silk stockings and dishes to the ladies and stuff to the kiddies at Saturday matinees. Not all the movies made money, but the candy counter made the theaters successful.

We once rented the Fox Theatre downtown to show a Hedy Lamarr movie — and she was naked! I later met her when she took tennis lessons here from my friend Carl Earn.

My brother Mac was appointed US ambassador to Spain — probably by Franklin Roosevelt, I'm not sure. Mac was married to actress Kim Novak for a time. He was a lot older than me and later developed Alzheimer's. I took care of him for 11 years.

I probably have been at Prentis a dozen years or more, but I'm not sure. I'm very bad with time.

My closest friend here at Prentis, Jackson Black, passed away a long time ago. Nobody here remembers him now. He was a communist and didn't believe in G-d. I believe in G-d and democracy, but we respected each other.

I've written a book. It starts with the Big Bang 13.8 billion years ago and goes up to the present time. I wrote it longhand about a dozen years ago and I have a lady typing it and then I'll get it printed.

Did you know that you and I are 1–4% Neanderthal in our DNA? The Neanderthals were bigger, stronger, and had bigger brains than us. They had the same culture as ancient man, the *Homo sapien sapiens*, but they were wiped out by them. The Neanderthals were peaceful. They never hurt anything.

Harry Krim, 102, lives at Prentis Apartments. He was a former movie theater master of ceremonies and Ford Motor Company inspector.

CHOOSING GRATITUDE
RUTHE LEVY

AWAKEN.
I am aware I am breathing... my eyes open... my heart beats... I feel pain and tingling all over, and I am grateful.

I AM OVERWHELMED WITH GRATITUDE FOR A NEW DAY, ANOTHER DAY.
An opportunity to exercise my G-d-given free will... to give and to receive... to live my purpose... to choose, and I am grateful.

I UNDERSTAND TIME IS A GIFT; THE EXTENT OF HOW MUCH TIME I WILL BE GRANTED I CANNOT KNOW.
I value the three hours it takes me every day to sit up, hang my legs over the side of the bed, eventually stand, ambulate, and accomplish my personal care, including getting dressed for the day... this is precious time, and I am grateful.

I HAVE A PLAN.
I plan life-sustaining measures (food, medication, movement, mental exercise, lifelong learning, interaction with others, including activities of interest, and volunteering), and I am grateful.

I FEED MY SOUL.
I pray, I connect spiritually, I attempt to live as best I am able to, acknowledging my missteps and striving to be better and to walk a "right path" — *derekh eretz* — and I am grateful.

I PURSUE MY OWN BRAND OF CREATIVITY.

I occasionally create delicious and colorful meals, bake delicious and eye-pleasing desserts, arrange home-sweet-home in a colorful, organized, and peace-inducing environment. I am aware that what I was able to create daily has necessarily been reduced from my past, yet I am grateful.

I PROVIDE MULTI-SENSORY STIMULATION TO MYSELF FOR ENJOYMENT AND GROWTH.

I enjoy auditory stimulation via music, sounds of nature, conversation, and more; visual stimulation via the printed word, books, works of art, nature, and more; tactile stimulation with some limitations set by the loss of feeling in my hands and more, and I am grateful.

I ACCEPT MY ABILITIES AS THEY ARE TODAY.

I am aware of what I am able to do, how much I am able to do, and when I am able to do it. I am aware of how different my abilities are from the past, as my many challenges have developed and increased over the past 13 years. I am aware that who I look like to others does not recognize these challenges that have a major effect on every moment. Yet, and still, I am so very grateful.

I APPRECIATE PEOPLE IN MY LIFE.

I treasure those who have touched my life, from birth until this very day — family, friends, colleagues, acquaintances, and sometimes even passersby. People have opened the door to emotion, strength, knowledge, common sense, sensitivity, perception, and quality of life. I appreciate the opportunity to both give and receive, and I am grateful.

• • •

AND I AM GRATEFUL FOR ALL OF THE ABOVE, despite some loneliness, frustration, and sadness; multiple spinal conditions, cardiac issues, neuropathy, food challenges, arthritis, mobility challenges, fall risks, and other medical conditions that require me to create accommodations and, in some cases, do not allow me to engage. *I am ever so grateful.*

I am grateful. As offered in the Hashkiveinu blessing of the Sh'ma, my nightly ask of my Lord, grant me the ability to sleep peacefully and awaken to life; I ask for G-d to watch over me and ask for G-d to spread over me the canopy of peace.

Ruthe, 72, lives at Hechtman Apartments. She worked as a special needs teacher and a social worker case manager and taught Hebrew school for 26 years. She is very close with her 13 nieces and nephews, is an avid reader, and a "forever" adult learner who is passionate about Judaism. She likes to write and used to enjoy embroidery, knitting, gourmet cooking, and baking.

IF THERE'S A WILL, THERE'S A WAY

PHYLLIS LEWKOWICZ

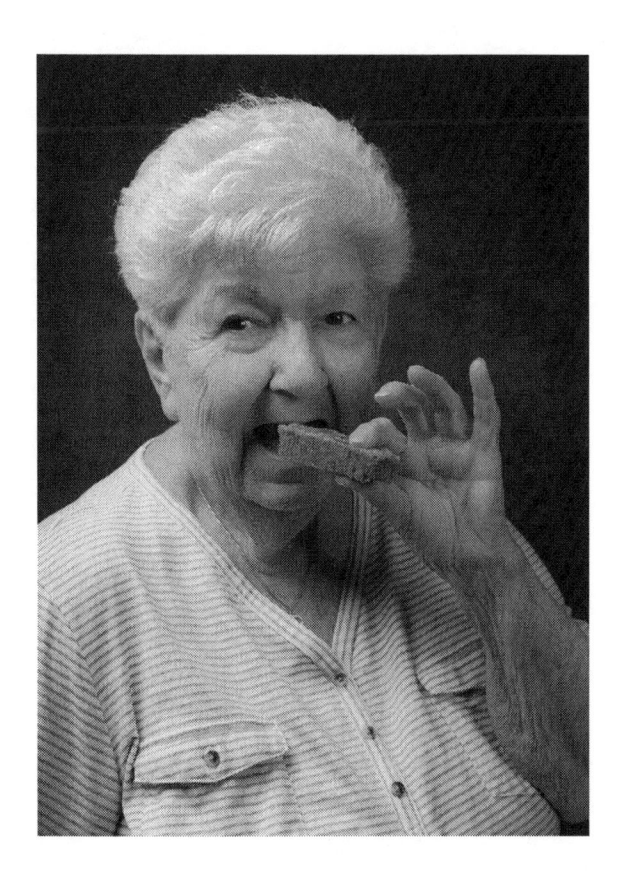

When I was five years old, I went to school and *learned* how to make friends. When I was 11, I *learned* "the facts of life." When I was 17, I got married and I *learned* how to be a wife. At 20, I had my first child and *learned* how to be a mother. My children grew up, married, and had children of their own. Joyfully, I *learned* how to be a grandmother. My husband died and at 62, I *learned* how to be alone. Most importantly, I *learned* that learning is knowledge, but experience is the teacher.

In January 2009, after recognizing I had a problem seeing, I was referred to a specialist, Dr. Darrin Levin. He diagnosed Age-Related Macular Degeneration (ARMD), a disease of the retina. I *learned* from his detailed explanation how my vision would continue to deteriorate. There is no cure for the disease and no specific treatment.

The next five years were an experience. My macular degeneration worsened, as expected. Much of what I enjoyed doing — sewing, knitting, crocheting, and especially reading — became next to impossible. Driving was limited to daylight hours. As if that wasn't enough, I came down with a virus that dramatically impaired hearing in my left ear.

Being a positive thinker all my life, I knew I had work to do. I took pride in my life's accomplishments as an independent, strong woman and moved forward, one step at a time. It wouldn't be long before I would have to stop driving. Changes had to be made, and I wanted to be the one to make them, on my own. I loved my Livonia home, but it was time to leave.

In September 2015, I put my house on the market and went looking for a new home. When my search was complete, I chose the Hechtman Apartments in West Bloomfield on the Jewish Community Campus. From the moment I walked into the building, I got a warm, friendly feeling, not only from the staff but the welcoming atmosphere. The list of amenities included was long, including transportation to doctors appointments and markets, dinner served in the dining room, special activities, and entertainment. The decision was made; I put my name on the waiting list.

I went home, called a realtor, and put my house up for sale. When I called my son and daughters to give them the good news, each said the same thing: they were happy I was moving. So was I.

Next, I packed. Two of my grandchildren came from Toronto to help, along with my daughter and son-in-law. What a blessing! We timed it perfectly. On December 17, 2015, I moved from the home I lived in and loved for 58 years. It sold on December 31, just days later.

As expected, my vision continued to deteriorate. Dr. Levin recommended a vision therapist, who led me to a path of new learning. At her suggestion, I contacted the Michigan Commission for the Blind and Visually Impaired. They sent the equipment I would need to listen to talking books, no charge. I received and returned books, and again, no charge. Now, I listen to about 20 books per month. I loved to read; now, I love to listen. Dr. Levin also facilitated the loan of an electronic magnifier.

The vision therapist also came to my new apartment and suggested color-coding buttons on the oven, microwave, and dishwasher. I couldn't see everything, but I could feel, and fortunately, my memory was okay. I *learned* so much from this experience, and I was grateful for the help.

The learning did not stop. I bought containers for my shoes and labeled them in large fonts with color and season labels. I arranged my clothing accordingly as well. I hired a carpenter to make shelves in the coat closet in order to properly organize my groceries. One of the other joys of my life was cooking and baking, and I had no intention of stopping.

There are about 200 residents at the Hechtman Apartments, and one of the things I love to do is entertain and feed my friends. My new mission was to make friends, and what better way to meet people than to feed them? The plan was to invite 25 residents to a delicious luncheon in the social hall. First, I sent a proper invitation. Many of my guests came dressed up. I served chopped eggs and onions, sesame pasta salad, tossed salad, kugel, crab salad, bread, crackers, mandel bread, tea, and coffee.

It was such a success that I did it again, invited more people, and made more friends. The more luncheons I made, the more friends I made. At Passover, I served sponge cake, wine and nut cake, brownies, and lemon puffs. My guests also enjoyed my not-so-high tea party.

One luncheon sticks out. A friend, Jerry Kurtis, asked everyone to raise their glass and said, "Phylis, we raise our glasses to you for the mitzvah you made by having us at this luncheon. Look around you, everyone has a smile on their face. Thank you." I was surprised and touched.

About six months after moving, I was forced to give up driving. It isn't easy to ask for help, but I *learned* to accept the generosity of others. With the help of my dinner companions, I contacted Debbie Cohn, and she became my eyes and ears and wheels. I don't know how I would manage without her. She does my shopping and takes me wherever I need to go, but best of all, she has become another daughter.

So many people ask how I am able to cook and bake if I can't see. My doctor said I would not go blind, I just wouldn't see well. He didn't say I couldn't cook or bake, so I *learned*. *If* there's a will, there's a way.

Phyllis, 88, lives at Hechtman Apartments. She had an extensive bookkeeping career and has served as president of both Congregation Beit Kodesh and their Sisterhood and the Livonia Group of Hadassah. She has three children, Mark Lewkowicz, Bonnie Lewkowicz, and Lisa Burk; seven grandchildren, Leah Lewkowicz, Joseph Lewkowicz, Samuel Lewkowicz, Sarah Lewkowicz, Cayla Burk, and Lindsey Burk; and one great-grandchild, Layla.

After her daughter Bonnie suffered a tragic accident that paralyzed her from the neck down, Phyllis not only worked to help Bonnie meet all her needs, but she also worked closely on the campaign for Barrier Free Design in Lansing, later known as The Americans with Disabilities Act (ADA). She currently makes greeting cards for the JSL community to raise money for the Hechtman Resident Council's flower fund, as well as the West Bloomfield Police and Fire Departments.

KINDERTRANSPORT
EDITH MANIKER

My name is Edith Maniker, but my name growing up was Edith Grunbaum. My parents, my older sister Paula, and I lived in Leipzig, Germany. As the Nazis gained more and more power and Jewish life in Germany was bleak, my parents saw an opportunity to save my sister and me.

England was taking in Jewish children from Germany, a rescue called the Kindertransport. In 1939, when I was just eight years old, I left by train for England on the Kindertransport. As I separated from my parents, to minimize the pain of our separation, my parents told my sister and me that we were going on vacation, and they would join us in two weeks. My sister Paula and I survived in England; tragically, my parents did not survive.

Among the heroic English families who took us in was Lady Clementine Waring in Devon. We had tea with her weekly and thought it was very funny to sing "My Darling Clementine." Shortly after our arrival, we were informed that we would not be allowed to sing that song while we were under Lady Waring's roof.

In July 1947, we left for America, my cousin, my sister, and I. We came to Detroit, where we had an aunt and uncle. After two weeks, we moved out. My sister and I both got jobs.

As an adult, I realized how brave my parents were to give their children up to total strangers. I felt that the world needed to know about the Kindertransport and parents like mine, and about the English families who provided safety for thousands of Jewish children. I felt a responsibility to talk about it, to teach and sensitize others, and especially to help students learn about what happened in the Holocaust.

I became a docent and a speaker at the Holocaust Center, where I spoke to countless groups of students about my experiences with the hope that they would learn to be respectful and tolerant of all minority groups. Sometimes, all they remembered of my talk was me and my sister singing "My Darling Clementine" to Lady Waring. But my hope is that students become more sensitive to the plight of others and do not succumb to hatred and prejudice. I am very touched by the letters that I've received over the years from students saying how special it was to have met me.

Edith, 92, lives at Meer Apartments, worked as a teacher's aide, and loves to bake. She has three children, Allen Maniker, Terry Tucker, and Marci Maniker-Leiter; four granddaughters, Lisa, Sarah, Mandy, and Ariella; and two great-granddaughters, Madison and Millie. Edith was honored as an 8 Over 80 Tikkun Olam Award recipient.

IT'S NOT RIGHT TO BURY A CHILD
CAROLE MASTER

The day we celebrated Susan Margarie Master Mendelson Goutkovitch's 60th birthday was also the day we got the news. We made a big deal out of birthdays and held a breakfast birthday party at Sunny's Cafe in West Bloomfield. I always made things fun, and I am so fortunate to have such a loving and wonderful family. Susan and her grandchildren live nearby, with lots of love and kisses and hugs and wrapping paper and cards.

Just as we got in the car to leave, her doctor called her with some terrible news: "*You have stage four pancreatic cancer.*" We were both in shock and the tears flowed as we embraced. This was October 11, 2022. We had no idea what the outcome would be. We chose to hope.

Susan and I were close. We practically grew up together, as I was only 20 when she was born. One of our most memorable mother-daughter trips was when we traveled through Europe in 1985, backpacking for two months on one of our crazy adventures, photographing cities and the many people we met along the way. We even went to nude beaches wearing only cameras around our necks. I will never forget those delightful times with her. I'm thinking of all the good times, like the way we spent every Sunday together practicing yoga with special music that inspired both of us.

Susan's love for her work at Jewish Family Service was second only to how much she loved her kids, grandkids, husband, brothers, and brothers' wives. She was loved by her colleagues at JFS and was presented with their highest honor, a lifetime achievement award, during a special ceremony before an audience of 200. Susan spoke from her heart to the crowd about how she felt, what she accomplished as a therapist, and what a gift it was to give to others. That's what she always told me: "Mom, you feel better if you give."

Susan gave so much to the world. Her social work brought her immense satisfaction. She was a yoga teacher, a special and loving daughter, sister, wife, mother, and grandmother. She was strong and so creative. She was also a videographer. Years ago, she and I had a business where we dressed in tuxedos to film and photograph b'nai mitzvah and weddings. She was also a weaver and a writer. She wrote a book for children to help them express their feelings. I hope to publish her book for her one day.

I often wished it was me who had her cancer. I've survived cancer twice. Once, when I was pregnant, I had melanoma in my eye. Now I can only see from the other eye, but I survived it. I'm strong. A second bout with cancer took away my breasts, but not my strength. I think I helped Susan stay strong, and I know she helped me too.

The entire family was in shock over Susan's diagnosis, but she immediately researched and found a wonderful Detroit oncologist, Dr. Philip A. Philip. I had never heard of him, but she believed in him, and he took very good care of her. She helped herself and us by taking charge of her treatment.

Susan tolerated three cycles of chemo, each time getting very sick and experiencing horrible pain. Dr. Philip gave her morphine so she didn't have to feel the pain. She would be very weak for a while and then, when the pain went away, he would take her off the morphine and she would used painkillers only as needed. We were hopeful. I anticipated her living through the end of the year and that we would celebrate her every moment, but her cancer progressed too quickly.

Dr. Philip said the main thing she should focus on was her family, and she should exercise and eat well and smile a lot. Her family made her smile. She was a bubbie, and I reaped the benefits of her grandchildren. She was very attached to her first grandchild, Ava, who is two years old. Susan took care of her for her first year and taught Ava to walk in puddles, throw rocks, and play. She also loved her playtime with Zoe and Lev, who live in New York.

Susan loved my cooking, but I don't cook anymore. I saved my recipes and gave them to my children. My granddaughter has them all, and she loves to cook too. The family loves my recipes for kugel and *kasha varnishkes* (bowties and fried onions), and I made them for Susan. At the end, she just took two bites and that was enough for her. I was so happy she did. She existed on protein shakes which she forced herself to drink until she finally lost her appetite.

I couldn't imagine my life without Susan, but here I am. We used to spend every Sunday together — "Sundays with Mama." She would come over and we would do yoga and stretch and go swimming and walk together. She was a strong swimmer and wanted to swim with me again, but it wasn't to be. What could I do? I felt so helpless.

I tried to stay positive and help her look for the good in every moment. I knew in my heart that we didn't have much time. She got the worst cancer possible and it spread everywhere, even into her lungs. She found it hard to breathe. I prepared myself, for I knew she was leaving us. I worried about her husband and children and how they would suffer.

I wanted to go to Susan in the hospital, but she didn't want me to see her in pain or to worry. It was very hard for me, especially when she couldn't talk to me about her condition. She lost her hair. We were all with her all the way.

It's so unfair what happens to cancer patients. We were all with her, holding her the day she took her last breath. And then we buried her. I will continue telling her story and telling her how much I love her.

I learned so much from Susan. I used to suffer from depression quite a bit, and I've always had therapy. As a therapist, Susan gave me tools to heal, like breathing exercises and suggestions for staying organized by creating schedules. She told me to make sure to do something good for myself and for somebody else every day. She reminded me to smile, to exercise, and to shower daily. I always say if you see somebody without a smile, give them yours. Susan did that, and I do that in her memory.

I'm very friendly. I love people, and I feel bad for the residents here who are depressed and ill. I always try to participate in activities at Hechtman. One thing that I love is playing Rummikub. I play almost every night, and it's very social. I play with five people, a tight group. We also go out to celebrate birthdays, play bingo, go to movies, and go to the exercise room. We try to stay positive.

Three years ago, I stopped driving because of the loss of my eye. Driving was a challenge, and I used to struggle a lot with it. When I gave it up, I had to depend on others. Fortunately, my partner Sandy drives. We enjoy going to visit our children, having family dinners, going shopping, and attending art fairs.

Losing independence is not easy, but I learned from Susan to move forward. I get joy from helping others. As a massage therapist, my clients would come to my home and I used to love giving them massages, which is a very loving therapy. I felt good about the work, and I know it helped others relax.

Susan had a lot to teach and taught her children and all those she touched many important life skills. Her children are brilliant, with great character and personalities. They are married and successful, and one of them is getting married in December (Dr. Avery Mendelson and Sarah Duffield). I had hoped Susan would be there.

I always say, "Every day is a gift." I wake up feeling blessed, and so I bless each day. We're lucky to be here, very lucky to be able to see the sunrise and the rainfall. It's important to be grateful for everything, to be here in this moment we are experiencing. Nothing else matters. I could die tomorrow, but I'm here now.

I will remember all the good things Susan and I shared. She gave me unforgettable years of love. Now our family tells her stories, and we love each other so much. She will never be forgotten. I listen to our music that we always listened to together, and she is with me. I will continue to share stories of her with her children and my friends. I will cherish her photos.

I used to paint pictures for her, which she said she "loved, loved, loved." On Friday, I'm going to my painting class. That's what Susan would have wanted. May her memory bless the lives of our family always.

Born in Montreal, Carole, 82, came to Michigan with her husband Eli in 1972 when he was transferred to Detroit to work as an engineer. An artist since kindergarten, Carole worked as a professional photographer, owned a greeting card business called The Bottom Line, and had one-woman shows in Birmingham and Saugatuck. She also worked as a massage therapist for 30 years.

Carole lives at Hechtman Apartments with her sweet companion Lacy, a Shih Tzu, and her partner, Sandy Tarnopol. Her greatest joys are her adult children, Susan (of blessed memory) and Coby Goutkovitch (who owns Coby's Judaica at the JCC), Neil and DeeDee, and Mitchell and Wendy; her nine grandchildren, Ali, Bradley, Ethan, and Jen, Avery and Sarah, Ben and Mary Tal, and Doug; and her five great-grandchildren, Ava, Sammy, Zoe, Lev, and Maatan.

A SEA OF SUPPORT
DEBBIE MERIN

My name is Debbie Merin and I'm 68 years old. I have always loved my dear family so much that I carry their photos with me every time I leave my home. I have wonderful memories of sharing special celebrations and holidays with them, along with living in South America. I experienced some painful times with peers who didn't understand my special needs and said cruel things that hurt my feelings.

My family tried their best to protect me and provide a wonderful and full life. But sadly, most of my beloved family has passed away, except for a loving sister and a cousin who lives out-of-state. Before they died, my parents connected me with the Jewish Association for Residential Care (JARC). They care about me and love me very much. I am part of the JARC family and have met many treasured lifelong friends through this organization.

We celebrate Jewish holidays; go to movies, theatre, festivals, and art classes; try out new restaurants; have picnics at parks, and more. Most importantly, I know that I'm beloved, thought of, and that others will always be there for me.

My biggest lesson as I've gotten older is learning that friends can help fill the void of losing so many family members. I'm grateful every day for my loving friends. They mean the world to me.

This is a snippet of Deborah Merin's life. She is 68 and grew up in a time when there were few services and supports for those with special needs. Often, those with intellectual challenges or emotional/mental issues never received services and were alienated from those around them. They were rarely invited to play with other kids or to attend parties, and often weren't treated with respect and kindness.

Some came from very loving and supportive families like

Debbie, while others ended up in hospitals as families couldn't deal with the challenges. As Debbie aged, most of her family members passed away. She had a few loving relatives who lived out-of-state. Her parents connected her with JARC decades ago, as they worried about what would happen to her once they passed away. JARC became her family and backbone, and her life is full of staff and JARC friends who care deeply about her welfare and love her dearly.

This was illustrated at a recent JARC-sponsored event, under a tent at a temple on a warm balmy night. Debbie often needs cajoling to try something new, or to go out of her comfort zone and take a leap of faith. This is likely due all the bullying and hurtful words she endured from other kids growing up, and from being ignored and misunderstood so often. But with a gentle push and a word of encouragement, a JARC staff member picked her up along with two peers.

At the event, she was with 100 others in a sea of support, welcoming words, smiles, and hugs, and she shined! The event included drumming on giant rubber balls and she totally got into it, hitting her drumsticks in time to the live musicians. She was smiling, joyful, and at peace. She also had a picnic of delicious foods and the company of other JARC members who treat her with loving kindness, warmth, and acceptance — the way we all need to be treated. That night was so special to Debbie, a highlight. She felt at home with her second family, and it is a treasured memory.

Shoshana Arden Rubenstein, ACSW

Debbie, 68, is a resident at Prentis Apartments, where her favorite activities are outings to restaurants, birthday parties, walks at the park, art fairs, and holiday celebrations, including the annual sukkah walk. She also loves music, arts and crafts of all kinds, knitting, and making homemade birthday and thank you cards.

ONE AND BE DONE
JILL MESSINGER

As I hung up the phone, I was confronted with what I thought would be a life-altering decision. I knew once I made it, just like jumping off a cliff, there would be no turning back. My surgeon of many years said, "This is it, Jill. Are you ready?" I paused, held my breath for a minute, and then said yes reluctantly, because I was scared!

I closed my eyes after we hung up, dropped the cell phone, and then the tears started coming like a big tidal wave. I was facing a leg amputation, something that most can't imagine.

The advantage for me was that it was a planned surgery that was always a possibility. I wasn't facing the kind of shock someone would experience from getting into a car accident and waking up to find their leg was gone with no warning. August 18, 2022, definitely changed my life.

I am now 59 years young, but going back to when I was 43, I had already been on dialysis treatment for 20 years and had been through many other medical issues as well — cardiac arrest, bladder cancer, lung surgery, and a failed kidney transplant, just to name a few. Then, when I turned 43, I was diagnosed with peripheral artery disease, a condition of poor circulation and narrowing of the arteries in the legs.

I had been faced with poor blood flow in my legs for 16 years and ended up wheelchair-bound, but I still managed to do well. I always kept my legs moving, stimulating blood flow.

Then, over a short period of time, I started feeling like a sinking ship. My toes started to deteriorate, and they weren't responding at all to podiatry or vascular care. I knew things were getting much worse because my toes began turning gangrenous. Before my blood could turn septic or toxic, my vascular surgeon said, "We have to do something, now."

I felt like things were spiraling out of control. The one thing that I feared might happen one day was coming true! There had been many blood flow interventions over the years, but now it was no longer possible to help the blood flow. The choice was between amputating my toes or doing an above-the-knee amputation. Of course, I thought about just taking the toes to put off the inevitable and keep my leg a little longer, sort of like a kid not wanting to part with a favorite blanket. That leg was my security and had been with me all my life!

I knew amputating the toes was very risky. There was a good chance the area would not heal well, making me prone to severe infection. I opted to do an above-the-knee amputation. I developed a slogan: instead of possibly multiple amputations, it was "one and be done."

Yes, I was scared. Even though I'd had numerous surgeries in my life, I just knew this one would be the most challenging. I had to prepare for it much like a boxer in the ring, getting as mentally tough as I could. I just knew I was not going to be defeated. But the unknown frightened me, especially not knowing what to expect when I got out of surgery. My surgeon advised me not to hide under my bed sheets, even though I was very scared to look down after surgery to see only one leg. It hit me like a ton of bricks: my leg was gone, actually gone.

After some physical therapy on the surgical floor, I moved up to the rehabilitation floor. They taught me so much in rehab. Maybe the supervisor of the department saw something in my energy and attitude that made her want to work with me personally, but she always referred to me as her rock star, her hardest-working student.

I thought I knew what I had to face, but I truly lost my confidence when I had to transfer. Lifting my body and moving from the wheelchair to the bed was a big task to accomplish supported by only one leg. I was so scared that I wouldn't be able do it that I would just sit in my hospital rehab room and stare out at space at night.

So many things I had been doing for years involved going from my wheelchair to my bed or the couch, or getting in and out of a car.

At one point, in my attempt to transfer to the bed from my

wheelchair, my arms were shaking badly. I yelled to the nurse, "Grab me now, I think I am going to fall!" But every day, and over time, my strength and confidence increased.

They taught me how to do things in the wheelchair like I did before. They tried to simulate the layout of my apartment so that when I went home, I could apply everything I had learned.

What a wonderful feeling to be home again and to challenge myself. I was so elated to be able to have that confidence back again in my own surroundings! I had caregivers to help me, but I quickly became very independent and saw that all the hard work in rehab had paid off. I just kept saying to myself, *You're doing it! You really are doing it!*

After a grueling three-week hospital stay, a wonderful feeling came over me as soon as I rolled through my apartment door. All my years of experience in the wheelchair had paid off. I knew exactly how to manipulate that chair. I knew the angles and the space I needed to transfer. I could even transfer to my bed with the lights out at night. I had never forgotten my skills — I just thought I had.

Once my confidence was there again, I was off and running. I knew I had what it took to persevere. I knew the future benefit of amputation totally outweighed the risk of the surgery. Finally, I had peace of mind — no more blood flow interventions needed. I came out fighting like a champ.

I have learned so much in my older years, especially about the importance of a strong, positive attitude, which is at least half the battle, and how important it is to never give up!

I opted not to get a prosthetic leg to help me walk again, but I didn't feel like I needed it because I could transfer everywhere so successfully.

The doctors and I felt strongly that I wasn't going to start walking after 12 years. The disease that put me in the wheelchair was still there, and there were no guarantees that months, maybe years, of painstaking effort would allow me to ever walk again.

That is okay, because I have returned to normalcy in so many ways.

I can go out shopping with friends, with my caregiver to the grocery store, sing in a choir, write poetry, go with my boyfriend to theaters, restaurants, concerts, and movies, join a temple and an amputee support group, and go on trips with residents in my apartment building. That scared little girl is no longer scared. I feel free like a bird, flying higher than I ever thought I could.

I have all the love and support in the world from friends, family, and caregivers, and I know I will continue to persevere and live my life to the fullest.

I know I will always be that fighter. Amputation saved my life without dampening my indomitable spirit.

Jill, 59, lives at Hechtman Apartments. Her professional background is sales, market research, and focus group recruitment. She loves singing, writing, wheelchair dancing, listening to music, reading, spending time with friends, watching old movies, musicals, and plays, eating out, doing adult coloring books, and watching concerts on PBS and YouTube.

ADELE NODLER

Recently as I approached the mirror,
And loudly said, "Now, how did I get here?"

The once-brunette hair so shiny and bright
Has turned to a stylish gray overnight!

It seems like only yesterday,
That I ran outside to play.

It all began in Detroit on Elmhurst Street,
Where life was so simple, fun, and sweet.

My four younger siblings were also born there,
It was where we learned many skills that we could share.

In that upper flat, in which, for many years, we did dwell,
Found our aunt, uncle, and cousins in the lower flat as well.

Together we attend school with pride and joy,
My cousins, siblings, three sisters, and one boy.

Our extended family was close at hand,
Having them nearby was special and grand.

Fortunately, some very special friends did come about.
Through our high school years, we did brag and shout,

"Through thick and through thin and even through fat,
Each of us knows where the other is at!"

In the blink of an eye, the years did fly fast,
And my college years were completed at last!

The years spent in the classroom were tricky, it's true,
Teaching was the career I enjoyed and loved to do!

A LOOK IN THE MIRROR
ADELE NODLER

A LOOK IN THE MIRROR

Once again, as I approached the mirror,
And loudly said, "Now, how did I get here?"

After years of dating Alvin, the wedding bells did chime,
Signaling the fact that I was his and he was mine.

Our union brought us many moments of pride and joys,
The best of these events were the births of our wonderful boys!

The years of raising them were delights to behold,
As they grew to mature both strong and bold.

Watching their achievements both night and day,
Absolutely, without question, blew our breaths away.

Here, again, as I approached the mirror,
And loudly said, "Now, how did I get here?"

During our 58 years of marriage, the challenges were there,
We climbed all those hills with laughter and care.

The marriages of the boys brought us such special pleasure,
An added dividend, our beautiful grandchild to love and treasure!

When his illness struck, the trails grew higher,
As we worked to provide his every desire.

Here, again, as I approached the mirror,
And loudly said, "Now, how did I get here?"

Being a widow brought with it another new concern,
There were many new lessons I would have to learn.

Many decisions I would now have to make,
Sell the house, downsize, and what to take?

ADELE NODLER

Here, again, as I approached the mirror,
And loudly said, "Now, how did I get here?"

A Jewish Senior Living facility was where I wanted to be,
After visiting Hechtman Apartments, I thought, This is for me!

Without the help of my children and grandchildren, it could not be done,
As they worked so hard to make the big move successful and fun.

After this move, my new life would have its start,
With activities for both my mind and my heart.

Meeting new people and having conversations galore,
I have found living here interesting and never a bore!

My new home also affords me the continued opportunity to volunteer,
With the organizations that to me are so very special and dear.

Here, again, as I approached the mirror,
And loudly said, "Now, how did I get here?"

I pray that G-d will give me the strength, so my life I will redefine,
To continue to make contributions, be happy, safe, and fine!

Adele, 81, lives at Hechtman Apartments. She is a retired teacher with two married sons, Harold (Leslie) Nodler and Michael (Dana) Nodler; two married grandchildren, Joshua (Becca) Nodler and Rachel (Danielle) Nodler; and two grand-dogs. She loves music, musical movies, and plays. She volunteers at Friendship Circle, Jewish Family Service, Jewish Hospice, and JARC. Adele enjoys reading, writing, crocheting, and being with her family.

TIMOTHY
DIANE PLISKOW

Hi! I'm Timothy the Cat, and welcome to my world.

My owner and I live at Prentis Apartments, and I have a secret: I love water! I don't mean just to drink. I like to play in the shower, especially when Diane is using it — only she is careful not to get me too wet. I can watch the water run from the hose until Diane tells me time's up and I go off on my own. Ask your pet, if you're lucky enough to have one, if he'd like to try this game. Have fun!

Here's my side of the story:

I was lucky enough to be given you as a foster pet when my friend Sharon could no longer care for you. You played, you ate, you slept, and you won my heart. When I was told you were to be up for adoption, Timothy, I knew I wanted you as my forever pet. It was put in writing one summer day in July at the Rochester Humane Society.

Happily, I took you to what is now our home, and soon you were playing with new toys galore.

My first inspiration was to give you a castle of your own, so I provided you with a condominium in the sky until it became just another item on which you could sleep, so we moved on to a more intellectually stimulating toy — a puzzle! The solution was moving the pieces until you found the ultimate reward — treats for you, Timothy, to eat.

I soon felt you were bored with this first game, so I purchased another similar game. It was obvious to me that it bored you even more; I was completely flunking the "Yay!" test.

Of course, there are always at least 10 tiny catnip-stuffed toy mice which continue to be batted around the apartment and are frequently lost and found again.

You are not just a playmate, Timothy, as you have become very attuned to my moods. Once, I was missing a friend who had been away for a while. I knew you understood me when you brought your favorite toy to me. When I tried to return it, I found it placed meaningfully in my bedroom.

On a lighter note, there's always the daily shower to play in with me, your ever-in-love-with-you owner. I love you furrever, Timothy!

Diane, 77, has lived at Prentis Apartments since 1982. She was born in Detroit and went to Mumford High School, where she played tennis on the tennis team. Diane loves to read, and her apartment is full of books. She also loves to paint and give her paintings to friends, most recently one of a cat.

THE WORLD: MY OYSTER
ROZ ROGERS

Remember *The Little Engine That Could*? Well, the reason he could was attitude. Keep a positive attitude, and you will have found the secret to maintaining a life well-lived.

My husband, Larry, and I were at a social event in 1976 when friends told us about their recently purchased travel agency. They invited me to join them as a travel agent in this exciting venture, and without hesitation, I jumped in feet first. This was my foray into a more-than-40-year love affair with fabulous travel experiences and an education that could not be offered in books.

The "I think I can" started with me mastering a new device called a "computer." It was very intimidating at first, but I gave it my all until I became comfortable with the challenge.

In 1979, China was opening to travel, and one of my coworkers and I jumped at the chance to be among those to enter this colorful world with so many interesting experiences. People were still wearing Maoist clothing and using ox carts; they looked at us as if we were aliens.

At a restaurant, we were served some small "ribs," and my friend made the mistake of asking what they were. Our guide informed us that they were mice, with the explanation that there are many mice in China: "Take broom, go *whop*, and cook." I instantly became a vegetarian and actually lost weight on that trip.

Also, when I asked the server how she knew the water was hot or cold, she stuck her finger in the thermos as a thermometer. The bathrooms were also "unique." They were holes in the ground, and squatting to pee was not easy to adapt to. Ah, memories. The hotel had straw mattresses and the heat had been turned off because March *was* spring! *Brrr!*

Another adventure was on a trip to East Africa, where our housing was quite primitive. Walking to the dining hall one evening, I encountered a herd of water buffalo, who fortunately decided we were not part of their menu that evening.

I have been to almost all the continents, though not Antarctica — too cold! Paris was a favorite trip, as were trips to London, Rome, Milan, and the French Riviera. A visit to the Taj Mahal was amazing.

My husband loved cruising; the longer the itinerary, the happier we were. Even an ocean crossing proved fun. I recall attending a scarf-tying class on board one cruise. Larry took a painting class and was going to make copies of his "art" so the kids could put something on *their* refrigerators.

These days, I find that I dream of travel, and I do enjoy the independence those experiences have given me.

I feel fortunate to be living at Hechtman. I am president of our resident council, participate in the Live Wire Choir and the readers' theater group, and lead Friday Shabbat prayers. I love it all.

There was a song by Johnny Mercer in 1944 called "Accentuate the Positive." That is the attitude that remains a part of my life. I know I am living a life well-lived. Lucky me!

Roz, 86, lives at Hechtman Apartments. She was born in Buffalo, New York, and worked as a travel agent for 40 years. She has three children, Shari Rogers, Neal Rogers, and Julie Kowalsky, and four grandchildren, Lucas, Louie, Lily, and Isaac. She loves music and going to see movies, theatre, and dance.

GRANDMA DOHERTY
ILENE RUBIN

Before moving to Meer, but after he was diagnosed with dementia, my husband Henry lived in a memory care community near our home in West Bloomfield. I visited him frequently. He was more himself when I was there. Two years after he was diagnosed, he passed away. We had been together a month shy of 66 years, and this was a big change for me. It was the first time I had truly been alone and had to make my own decisions.

Although my children were always there to help me, they never pushed me into anything. I stayed in our large condo until I made the decision to move to Meer. I knew some people at Meer who highly recommended it. I knew folks at Fox Run and All Seasons, but those places weren't right for me. When the time came to decide which senior community I wanted to live in, I knew I wanted a place where there was a good feeling of being part of the Jewish community — and most importantly, where they served kosher food.

I wanted a two-bedroom apartment on the first floor, and one month after I added my name to the list to move into Meer, a two-bedroom apartment became available. I knew that was it. It was just exactly what I wanted, and I didn't hesitate. I asked myself, *What are you waiting for?*

When I got there, I wanted to do more than just sit in my apartment. Meer was opening the Krohlik Café and requested residents and volunteers to operate it. I was the only resident who responded. I volunteered twice a week and was so happy to get to see people, feed them, and visit with everyone. I became a spokesperson and an ambassador for Meer. Whenever prospective residents were touring the building, I would tell them how much I loved living here. So many of my old friends whom I hadn't seen since high school now live at Meer. I'm very happy here.

Helping out is something I have always done since I was a little girl. I walked a little boy with special needs to school and would walk him home afterwards. During the war, I volunteered at the rationing board in Highland Park, where I handed out coupons. I volunteered at the Shubert Lafayette Theater as an usher. I babysat my nephew and volunteered at the Red Cross blood bank. Both my husband Henry and I loved to volunteer together, and we did this after we were married through the time our children were grown.

When we moved from Detroit to Farmington Hills, we spent time volunteering at Gill Elementary School, and then, when I moved to West Bloomfield, I volunteered at Doherty Elementary School. The kids didn't know who I was, so I told them, "While you are in school, I'm your grandma." So I became Grandma Doherty. I was there for 16 years, and shortly after I moved in, a young man working at the Meer front desk recognized me as Grandma Doherty. He remembered drawing a picture for me.

Living at Meer keeps my mind active, and I love engaging in so many of the activities with my friends at my side. Life is good.

Ilene, 93, lives at Meer Apartments with old friends and new friends. She was born in Detroit and raised in an Orthodox home. She became a secretary for the servicemen's bureau during WWII, where she represented veterans and helped them fill out their forms to get benefits. She loves classical music, especially Beethoven and Strauss, and played the violin.

Ilene learned how to use a computer and iPad to get the news and checks her emails daily to stay in touch with family and friends around the world. She has three daughters, Cynthia Howard, Sheila Graziano, and Marilyn Rubin; two grandchildren, Alana and Ezra; and one great-grandson, Lorenzo.

FLY GIRL
TERRI SILBERSTEIN

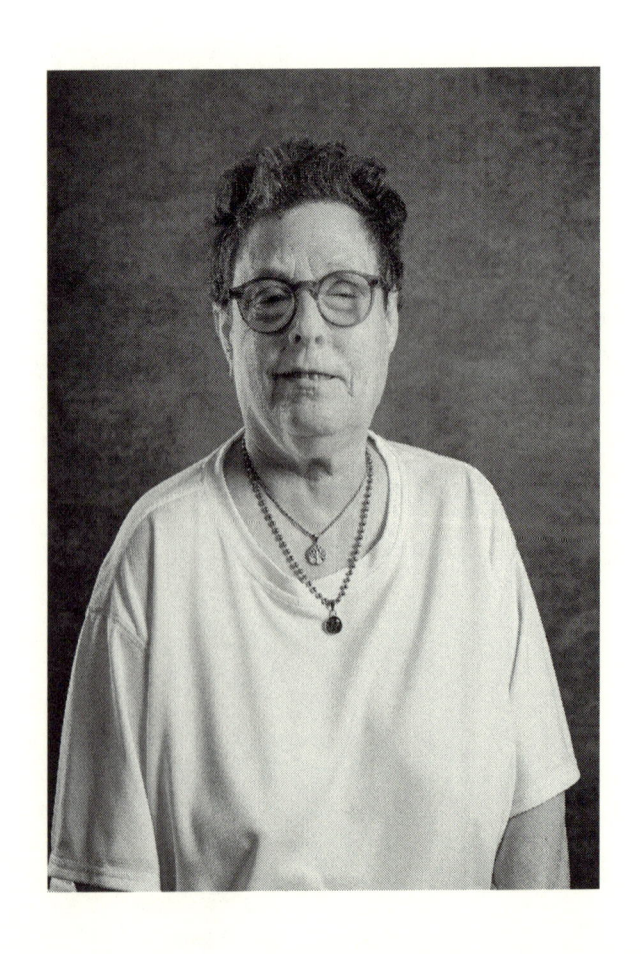

I've always been a thrill seeker and always thought about skydiving. I finally decided to do it, but I wanted to know everything about it, from what it felt like to what the best place was. After two years of research, I found the place, Bucket List Skydiving, and signed up. I wanted to dive through the clouds, so I decided to try it. I was very nervous when I got there, but I said to myself, *OK, I can do this. These people are professionals. They know what they're doing.*

When I got there and was walking to the plane, I noticed some rust on it and asked my instructor, "How old is this plane?" When he told me it was 25 years old, I started to pray! The plane was extremely loud and rattled a lot. My heart was racing. Inside the plane, there were no chairs. I had to sit on the floor and there was no door. I had to move to the edge of the plane with my instructor, and then I was out.

When I first jumped out of the plane, I was free-falling at 120 mph with my instructor strapped to my back. The wind was so loud and the G-forces were at seven — which is high — pulling the skin on my face back. To my surprise, I didn't feel a thing! Later, I saw myself on video, and I looked like the Creature from the Black Lagoon.

The view was amazing. The sky was so blue, and the earth below was so green. Flying through the clouds was amazing, just like flying through the air. I didn't feel them, but I could see them, and when both chutes opened up, what a difference! It became so quiet. My instructor, Joel, handed me what looked like two dog leashes to steer the parachute to the left and to the right.

Finally, after eight minutes, it was time to land, and it was a lot smoother that I thought it would be. In order to land, I put my legs straight out in front of me. I was in a seated position along with my instructor. After I landed, I stood up and raised my arms in the air and screamed, "I did it!" I went over to Joel and gave him a big hug.

I highly recommend skydiving to folks who are not afraid of heights. It is a head-rush I will never forget. In fact, I went back for a second jump. My new friend Joel calls me "fly girl." I love that name!

Terri, 70, has lived at Prentis Apartments for seven years. She was born in New York City but has lived all over the country, and has worked as a medical assistant, home remodeler, and tennis instructor. Her hobbies include skydiving, playing chess, biking, tennis, and drumming. She leads a drum circle at Prentis.

THE GIFT OF ART
ANN SPENCER

Hi, my name is Ann, and I just want to say I feel that I have lived a hard life, but a life ultimately well-lived!

At two-and-a-half years old, I contracted polio from walking through puddles in the street gutters. My mom and dad had left each other when I was just a baby, so I didn't really know my dad. I did come out of the polio from the hospital on my own two feet, but I had a foot problem and needed several surgeries on my foot and Achilles tendon to walk flat. I was in and out of school a lot to get it worked on, so I missed a lot of school, got behind, and was put in remedial classes, so I got picked on a lot. But I still got a diploma at 17 years of age, and I was not living at home at the time.

My mother was working as a waitress, taking care of me and my younger sister, and having a hard time. One day, she said, "I can't support both of you, and one of you will have to go," and that one was me. I was on my own. Homeless. I lived in the park in Wyandotte where the Boblo Boat came in.

When I was in school, I had an art class. Kids would ask me to paint on their faces or arms — peace signs, flowers, and things like that. Then they wanted me to give them tattoos in ink. That was something I could have gotten in trouble for — but I didn't, and the kids really liked them. I didn't want to get in trouble though, so I had to stop to avoid getting caught.

I got a C+ in art. I was upset about it and didn't do art for quite a while. After that, a lot happened. I graduated from high school and tried to go back home, but my mom said no, so I left the state and went from place to place. I met my first husband, was with him for 13 years, and had a baby. Then, my husband started using intravenous drugs, and so I left him.

I was having my own struggles with alcohol and pills, so I left my son with his grandmother and went into the army for a year. When I got out, I came back to Michigan to see my family, whom I had not seen for 10 years. I stayed with my sister; then, my mom and her husband, who I had never met, took me in for a few months. My son, who was six, came to live with us. I had a lot of growing up to do and my mother and I were not getting along, so she kicked me out again.

I was homeless off and on, but I made it through and tried to do better to take care of myself. I met my second husband, got married, and had a daughter with him. By the time she was five or six, his physical abuse escalated to the point where I knew I needed to get divorced.

It had been a hard road, and I changed my life for the better after that. I stopped hitting the bars and started going to church and changing my lifestyle. I knew that the road I was on wasn't any good for me or my children. I knew I needed to make a change, and I did.

By my determination, I was able to create a life well-lived. I found myself at a senior center doing a few paintings and gradually expanded my artwork. Now, many years afterward, I find myself where I am comfortable — because of my art and what I believe are miracles from G-d, who has helped me a lot and who I believe is looking out for me. I've been painting nature, G-d's creation, trees, flowers, and landscapes.

There are people who have helped me a lot with my art. I've learned from looking at the art of people like Thomas Kincaide, Bob Ross, and Vincent Van Gogh, and some really good people I have taken classes with. I hope people can get as much out of looking at my art as I do, because it makes me feel happy inside.

Thank you for reading about my life. I hope some of it helped you as well. Don't give up on your dreams, because they will keep your heart happy. G-d bless.

Ann, 73, lives at Hechtman Apartments. She has two children, Scotty and Alisha. She is still actively creating artwork, primarily painting and making jewelry. She loves to sing and regularly attends karaoke. Whatever they've got going on, she's into it, she says.

TINY TREASURES
ANN TORF

An old, rumpled brown grocery bag holds some the most treasured items I possess. The bag sits next to the lounge chair in my living room at Hechtman Apartments. Each day I reach into the bag and pull out cards and letters sent to me from friends and relatives all over the country. They started to arrive right after the first of the year in 2023. My daughter, Cheryl, had sent out an email announcing my upcoming 95th birthday. I'm a Valentine's Day baby.

Until the mail started pouring in, I hadn't realized how many lives I'd touched. My family was always close knit. I was one of three sisters. Our husbands called us "The Three Musketeers." We had the good fortune to marry men who became friends. After living in Detroit until the early '50s, we moved to Oak Park, all of us.

We lived no more than a couple of blocks from one another. Our children grew up in each other's homes, 12 first cousins in all. My husband Jack and I had five, including a set of twins. We were part of the post-war expansion to suburbia, but our traditional ideals stayed intact. Holidays were observed. Sunday night dinner at my sister's was non-negotiable. One of our favorite meals was barley soup and hamburgers.

We had a big family that always included others. You didn't have to be related by blood. We welcomed everyone. In a card from Felicia, my brother-in-law's niece, she confessed she had a hard time believing she wasn't related to her wonderful "An Tanny":

> You always showed me love, allowing me to feel okay. You were just a kind person, but it was always way more to me. Do you know what you mean to me?

I smile to think about it. They used to call me "The Mom of Everyone." In a note from one of Cheryl's friends, she recalled our lively household full of fun and delicious tuna salad. Another card says:

I'm grateful for you and all the ways my life is better because you're a part of it.

We celebrated my 95th birthday, starting on February 12th and continuing through the 19th. My children came from everywhere: Howard from Hawaii, Mark from Boise, Gary from Denver, Andrea from St. Louis, and of course, Cheryl from right here in Farmington Hills. I beam with pride — all college graduates. There must have been close to 50 people, including nieces, nephews, grandchildren (I have eight of them), friends, and neighbors.

It was a wonderful week, and I'll never forget it. Every day, I dip into my rumpled, brown paper bag and reach in for a dose of happiness and joy and kindness. That's the best medicine there is. And the cards keep on coming. There are well over 100 now.

Ann, 95, was born and grew up in Detroit, where she bowled in the B'nai B'rith bowling league and occasionally worked as a bookkeeper. She has five children, Cheryl Ceifetz, Howard Michael Torf, Mark Torf, Gary Torf, and Andrea Torf; eight grandchildren, Andrew, Marla, Ryan, Ira, Gavriel, Adina, Mira, and Carolyn; and four great-grandchildren, Julia, Sloan, Harry, and Alessandra. Ann's favorite activity is seeing her grandchildren and great-grandchildren.

MOVED BY THE WORD OF G-D
REGINA TURNER

I am a person of deep religious faith. I have experienced G-d's work in my own life in what He did for me and with my son and my nephew.

As a divorced single mother, I faced challenges because my son had delayed development. I was fortunate to have the support of my parents. They bought me a house so I could work to support my son and, with G-d's guidance, get him the help he needed. We did Head Start, worked with a speech therapist, and more, all the time praying for healing.

Specialists told me he would never improve, but I always told him he could do all things through G-d, who strengthens him. And my son has thrived. He now has a driving job and just passed his test for a commercial driver's license so he can get a better driving job. He has a fiancée and a new daughter on the way. My friends and family say I did an extraordinary job with him, but I give all credit to G-d, who guided me.

I also count on G-d's help with my great-nephew who lost his father at a very young age. My niece and her husband had two children, my great-nephew and great-niece. My niece's husband passed suddenly at age 30 in the presence of his son. The boy was so traumatized that he developed a stutter. G-d has shown us the way to get him help to cast away the stutter. I bought children's Bible story DVDs and Bible songs on CD for him, and encouraged him to put himself in G-d's hands. We are praying for him and seeing some improvement.

I am blessed to have experienced the power of G-d in my life and in my loved ones' lives. I have seen how by supporting and helping each other, we do G-d's work, to the glory of G-d, our heavenly Father. I want everyone to know G-d shows us His goodness through His mercy, His grace, and His love.

Regina, 61, has lived at Prentis Apartments for four years. A native Detroiter, she worked as a medical assistant. She has one son. She loves to bake, and her family particularly loves her apple and peach pies and her homemade fruitcake for the holidays. Regina finds comfort in her deep religious faith. Her favorite passage of scripture is Romans 8:28: "And we know that all things work together for good to them that love G-d, to them who are the called according to His purpose."

HOW I MET MY HUSBAND
DEBBIE WARNER

HOW I MET MY HUSBAND

My first date with my husband was very funny. The doorbell rang and I opened the door to see Skippy there. I told him I had a blind date with a guy Eddie Supowitz fixed me up with named Leon Warner, and that he should go. His response was: "I am your date, Leon Warner." I had only known him as Skippy. He showed me his driver's license and we went out twice and the rest is history.

Skippy taught school in Allen Park, Michigan for 38 years. After our marriage and kids, I went to work for a friend from Mumford High School and became his insurance secretary and office manager for 28 years.

I moved to Meer from my condo in Farmington Hills, because before that, if I wanted to see my friends Ralph Woronoff and Rena Tepman, I had to drive miles to see them. At the time, I had broken my foot (the right one, of course) and couldn't drive. I came to see Jackie, who showed me a few apartments with my daughter Stephanie, and we decided on which one I needed. I moved at the end of March 2022.

Rena, Ralph, and I have been friends since I was 12 years old. Ralph was Skippy's cousin and stood up at our wedding.

I love the camaraderie at Meer. I always say, "Hello, how are you?" I love to go to the entertainment here, listen to lectures, and go to markets and Schoolcraft concerts. I play Rummikub, Canasta, and, of course, support Monday Night Bingo. I have made new friends and enjoy my time with them.

The longevity of my friendship with Rena and Ralph goes back over 65 years. Through thick and thin, sadness, and a lot of good times, we were there for each other. Skippy and Rena's husband Jerry went for physicals for the army together holding hands, because Jerry couldn't see without glasses. Finally, they were both rejected.

This year, as our dining room servers were graduating high school and leaving for college, we honored them with a prom. To my surprise, a gentleman named Steven Harp, a server, selected me to be his prom queen. So, whenever anyone says, "Hello, Queen," I give them my queen wave.

I love it here.

Debbie, 85, lives at Meer Apartments. She has four children, Jan Warner, Scott Warner, Pamela Marsh, and Stephanie Wagner, and six grandchildren, Kayla, Ian, Ella, Jack, Sari, and Eli. She loves to read, knit, socialize, and play Canasta, Rummikub, and mahjongg.

MY FRIEND'S FRIENDSHIP WITH HASHEM
LAURA M. WATSON

I have lived at Prentis for three-and-a-half years. It has been a pleasure to live here. The environs are very peaceful and serene, and the campus well-kept. The garden where we grow our vegetables to give to Yad Ezra is amazing.

I met Rabbi Yosil Rosensweig in his first class on Hebrew Scripture here at Prentis. I always wanted to know more, so I went. He was very warm and very inclusive, and that won me over. And he was very informative.

He felt that it was a divine calling to teach and that HaShem was watching him, so he typed out our lessons with great clarity and with a passion for encouraging us to love the Torah and learn wisdom. My revered friend Rabbi Rosensweig taught me many beautiful things about life:

1. The value of forthrightness.
2. The freedom a sense of humor brings.
3. The divine thread of mercy that shimmers and glistens in the darkest circumstances when exercised.
4. Honor of and respect for people of different cultures and nationalities.
5. Teaching is eluded and exemplified 90% through example and 10% through words.
6. Forgiveness and forgiving allow us space to breathe and think without overbrimming with self-pity, hatred, and bitterness.
7. Inclusiveness is a redemptive antibiotic against loneliness, rejection, despair, and hopelessness.
8. Love is when you share yourselves and your energy passionately and sacrificially to shield, protect, admonish, strengthen, and encourage others to persevere and to be the best people they can be.

Rabbi Yosil Rosenzweig, may he continue to be of blessed memory, opened a new door to life and the beauty of G-d.

My time here in Oak Park (which I affectionately call Jacob's Land, because Jacob's name was changed to Israel and there are many sects of Judaism in Oak Park) will be remembered as an experience that has allowed for growth, beautified my soul, and nurtured camaraderie and unity in communicating with people.

Laura, 74, lives at Prentis Apartments. She has one son, Shalom J. Watson. She worked in the post service for 25 years and published a book titled Blue Rose. *Laura has done all kinds of artwork, including sketching, watercolors, acrylics, ceramics, and calligraphy. She likes to walk, write, and visit patients at the hospital, where she prays for their health. Laura intends to live to 104 years old with clarity of mind, sharpness, and good health!*

GETTING BACK UP
SHEBA ZIETCHICK

love to walk. One day, as I was going into Meer, I tripped and fell and broke my wrist. Everyone said, "You are so lucky," because it was the left hand and I am right-handed. True though that may be, they didn't have to face the challenges I did. I invite anyone to try the following with one hand:

1. Opening toothpaste, vitamin bottles, or a jar of applesauce.
2. Making the bed.
3. Dishing out Cheerios onto a plate and pouring juice into a cup.
4. Washing the dishes.
5. Getting dressed (using the right hand to take off a garment was easy, but putting it on with the left hand in the cast was not).

I learned to overcome my temporary disability by not being dependent, and that's the way life is. Try to be busy, stay active, eat well, and continue to exercise. Life at Meer is indeed an experience, but a good one.

Sheba, 88, has lived at Meer Apartments for nine years. Originally from New York, she worked in accounting, at a school for emotionally disturbed children, and in a hospital office. She has three daughters, Wendy, Tandy, and Bonnie; 11 grandchildren, Shoshanna, Aviel, Shearer, Aviva, Caitlin, Jared, Tyler, Dillon, Jake, Nicole, and Christopher; and seven great-grandchildren, Shmuli, Mariam, Mosha, Liora, Maya, Chloe, and Yuval.

Sheba loves to walk and has travelled around the US and the world. Sheba considers herself a people person, but when she's alone, she likes to curl up with a good book. Her motto is, "Good, better, best — never let it rest until the good is better and the better is best."

FITNESS, BODY AND SOUL
MILLIE FRIEDMAN ZIVOV

My legal name is Mildred, but I like to be called Millie. I was born in 1929 and lived and grew up in Detroit. I am proud to say I learned how to use computers after taking courses in 1986 at OCC. For many years I was a secretary in a law firm. I worked for attorney Harvey Altus, who became like a son to me. My husband and I had two dogs over the years, Sir Lancelot, a Sheltie, and a poodle named Muffin of Drury Lane when we lived in Southfield. My favorite performer was Elvis Presley. I love his music — "The Wonder of You."

I've been a fitness advocate since I joined Vic Tanny's in Dearborn many years ago. Years ago, I felt frumpy and miserable, and exercise changed my life. Since I began exercising, I never stopped. It's a priority for me to work out and eat healthy foods. I love doing yoga and walking. I have also taken up Falun Dafa, based on the universal principles of truthfulness, compassion, and forbearance. I learned this peaceful practice from a Chinese man at Drake Park, where I go on Saturday and Sunday mornings. I get energy, feel relief from stress, and have peace of mind doing it. I also learned about Kangen water filtration, which uses electrolysis to create hydrogen-rich water, and use this apparatus in my apartment.

I've been on my own ever since my husband passed away. My son Greg lives in Houston and has two children, Stephanie, 42, and Brad, 39. My daughter Julie and her husband David live nearby. We are very close.

One day, a friend casually invited me to join her at an open house at Hechtman. I was 88 at the time and my daughter didn't think I was ready to move, but we still went to the open house. When I took the tour, I was shocked. I didn't expect it to be so adorable and so welcoming. I told my daughter, "I have made up my mind, and I would like to move to Hechtman." It was that quick. It was a feeling — a good feeling. I had just been diagnosed with cancer and decided to sell my condo, and now here I am, and I love my apartment.

I have a busy life at Hechtman. I am never deprived of socializing. I love meeting new people and being with old friends from Detroit I haven't seen in maybe 50 years — now, they are showing up in my life again at JSL. The best parts of my day are all the activities and seeing people who have become my dear friends. So much coming and going, the wonderful trips that we have to museums, and helping with classes as a volunteer. It's mind-boggling, it really is. I mean, I'm doing things I never thought I could do, and I am happy on the shuttles with my friends, going here and there and knowing my daughter doesn't have to worry, and I don't have to rely on her to take me places.

I volunteer at Hechtman, helping in the beading classes; I never realized that I had a knack for it. I learn from my new friends, like resident Phyllis Lewkowicz. She is sight-impaired and never complains. She does so much for others. I feel reconnected to life because of her and find it so interesting that even with her physical disabilities, she lives fully. I am completely inspired. I enjoy being with her and so many others.

My back occasionally hurts now, but I won't give up. Yoga was so important to me that I brought in a new yoga instructor to Hechtman. She is from India. I met her when I used to practice at the JCC. She is amazing and all the residents love her. I use the elliptical machine in the wellness center, and I can do it for a half hour without pain. My brother Harold has moved into Hechtman after having lived at All Seasons with his wife, who died recently. I'm so happy we will be together again. It will be wonderful and soothing for us to grow old together in a place that is so perfect. I love it here.

Millie, 94, lives at Hechtman Apartments. Born in Detroit, she was a legal secretary for over 24 years. She has three children, Greg Zivov, Julie Peven, and Rod Zivov (of blessed memory); two grandchildren, Brad and Stephanie; and three great-grandchildren, Madison, Frankie, and Theo. She likes watching Hallmark movies, playing mahjongg, exercising, and reading fiction and biographies. She particularly loved Unthinkable *by Jamie Raskin.*

THE GREAT WHITE HUNTER
AL ZLATKIN

THE GREAT WHITE HUNTER   137

My daughter came to visit me here in the Teitel Apartments in Oak Park about three years ago with a request. She asked if I could watch her dog, because she was going to have a few medical tests at the hospital. I readily agreed because I had not had the companionship of a dog for more than 20 years; back then, I owned, raised, and trained a number of Irish Setters.

So, she went back to her car and returned with her dog on a leash and two bags containing food, toys, and supplies. The dog was small and all white. He had a black nose and dark eyes. She told me he weighed about eight pounds and was a mix between a miniature poodle and a Maltese. She said his name was Frosty, and she called him Frosty the Snowman.

Frosty settled in pretty quickly. He was very quiet and found a place to rest under a chair in the living room of my apartment. His eyes followed me as I moved around.

Since I live on the ninth floor of the Teitel apartments, my first job was to teach Frosty to be potty-trained here. Putting a pee pad in the shower and showing him how to use it didn't work. I realized I would have to take him outside every four or five hours to do his business. This also helped him get used to his new environment. Now, he loves to go for walks. He'll decide the route, depending on what he needs to do. We usually go between the apartments and Temple Emanu-El next door.

One evening, we were out walking when Frosty pulled away and went into the bushes. He came back carrying a little baby bunny very gently, taking care not to hurt it. He let me take it, and we went back to the apartments. A friend happened to be outside and took a picture of Frosty, the Great White Hunter, with me and the bunny. I ultimately took the bunny back to where Frosty had found it in case its mother returned, but I keep that picture on my desk to relive the memory of when Frosty became the Great White Hunter.

PS: My daughter is now taking care of her mother, so it looks like Frosty and I are buddies for the long term, to my great delight.

Al, 84, is a lifelong Detroiter and has lived in Teitel Apartments for seven years. He worked in sales and raised and field-trained Irish Setters. He has two daughters, Cece Zlatkin and Sharon Zlatkin. He loves going fishing and taking care of his dog, Frosty.

ACKNOWLEDGMENTS

So many people worked together to put this volume together. We are deeply grateful to all of them for making this happen.

The book committee is a group of expert writers and editors who volunteered to interview, write, rewrite, and edit these pieces. This book absolutely could not have happened without them and their expertise. *Toda raba* and *yasher koach* to:

Elizabeth Applebaum
Shari Cohen
Shelli Dorfman
Alan Hitsky
Nicole Lupiloff
Sy Manello
Hannah Moss
Wendy Robins
Jo Rosen
Phyllis Schwartz
Dr. Charles Silow

The portraits of the writers in this book are each worth way more than 1,000 words. Photographers Ira Goldberg and Jon Lybeck volunteered to illuminate this volume with their immense artistry. They sat with each of the writers and got to know them before creating and editing the beautiful portraits in this book.

Lives Well Lived chair Hannah Moss is dedicated to Jewish

Senior Life and the FRIENDS mission. Each year, she comes up with a new and wonderful way to support and recognize our residents and older adults in general (in addition to doing a ton of work!). Her passion is the driving force behind this book.

No big project happens without the support of the entire agency. Thanks to Nancy Seigel Heinrich's inspired leadership as CEO, Jewish Senior Life is a place where ideas and creativity always have a place, and collaboration is our norm.

Special thanks to Jo Rosen, Executive Director of Development, for unwavering support and enthusiastic participation.

Thank you to development associate Beth Tryon, for always graciously helping with everything, and knowing everything about everything!

And, as always, thank you to the administrators, program staff, and desk staff at each building who helped facilitate each step of this project and everything else we do here!

Thank you all — thank you!

CREATIVE TEAM

ELIZABETH APPLEBAUM

Elizabeth Applebaum, who studied political science as an undergraduate at Stephens College and English Literature in the master's degree program at Hebrew University, has worked at *The New Orleans Times-Picayune*, *the Kansas City Jewish Chronicle*, *the Detroit Jewish News*, and the Jewish Federation of Metropolitan Detroit. She and her husband Phillip have four children and live in Oak Park. Elizabeth's favorite hobby is reading — especially about WWII, and preferably something focusing on her heroes Winston Churchill and fellow Missourian Harry Truman.

SHARI COHEN

Shari S. Cohen is a professional communicator with extensive experience in corporate communications and journalism, including managerial positions at the Detroit Medical Center and Comerica. She is a contributing writer for *the Detroit Jewish News* and has received multiple awards for her articles from the Detroit Chapter of the Society of Professional Journalists. Shari co-authored *Legacy of Excellence: A continuing history of Jesuit and Mercy higher education in Detroit*. She has been a reading tutor at Pasteur Elementary School in Detroit since 2009.

Late in 2021, Shari started a Creative Writing Group at Meer Jewish Senior Life. She is amazed and inspired by the response from the participants. Their creativity, willingness to try new things, and writing skills inspire her every week. In addition, the group has been a catalyst for developing new friendships.

IRA GOLDBERG

Ira Goldberg is the founder of Specialized Photographic Services, LLC in Farmington Hills, Michigan. Ira specializes in portraits, headshots, and brand photography. At his core, Ira is a people person and dedicated much of his life to building relationships, first as a teacher at Berkley High School and later as a photographer.

As a teacher, his desire was to help and watch students grow; as a photographer, his desire is to build a relationship of trust with his clients, resulting in creating images that tell their stories. Ira also believes that creating beautiful imagery with a client is lending power to their voice:

> "I want everyone to know that regardless of what stage of life they're in, they have purpose and beauty within. My objective with every individual that sits in front of my camera is to reveal that purpose and beauty and reflect it in an image they can be proud of."

For Ira, photography is a passion that dates back to his bar mitzvah, when his parents gifted him his first camera, and has only grown stronger over time. While the technology has certainly changed over the years, his drive to further develop his craft hasn't. Beyond photography, Ira loves to travel with his wife Nancy, spend time with their two cats, Gabriella and Tabitha, and find new ways to continually repurpose his life. He is excited to explore his new hobby of pizza baking.

ALAN HITSKY

Alan Hitsky is the former associate editor of *the Detroit Jewish News*, where he worked from 1974 until 2011. He and his wife Deborah were married at Congregation B'nai Moshe in 1971 and have been members of the synagogue for 52 years. He has served on B'nai Moshe's executive board, board of directors, and social action and ritual committees.

Alan was a Maccabi Club volunteer when the local Jewish Community Center hosted the youth games. He was treasurer of the Pet-A-Pet Club for 10 years and has served as treasurer of his Southfield neighborhood association since 2006. He has been a weekly volunteer at the Yad Ezra kosher food bank since 2011.

NICOLE LUPILOFF

Nicole Lupiloff is currently the Development Manager at Jewish Senior Life. She has 15 years of writing, editing, project management, communications, and administrative experience. In her spare time, she enjoys movies, tennis, and being with friends and family. Born and raised in metro Detroit, she currently resides in Midtown Detroit with her fiancé, Dana.

SY MANELLO

Sy's careers have been twofold. He taught English and public speaking in the Detroit School System for 30 years. He then went to work for *the Detroit Jewish News* and has been there for 35 years. He has a column that runs once a month, and he processes all of the milestone announcements.

In 2014, he began as a volunteer for JSL, working at Fleischman Residence. He calls bingo, serves afternoon snacks on Tuesdays, and reads aloud once a month. His reading "program" has since extended to Meer and Coville.

Sy has been recognized for his work by being elected a volunteer of the year and being an 8 Over 80 Tikkun Olam Award recipient.

HANNAH MOSS

Hannah began volunteering in the mid '80s at Borman Hall. She spent many years volunteering as a fund raiser with JARC and Maimonides Medical Society. She has been married to Gordon Moss for 49 years, raised two loving daughters, Jo and Kate, and is blessed with four grandchildren, Evie, Leah, Noam, and Talia. Hannah enjoys art and is currently writing her own memoir.

WENDY ROBINS

Wendy was born in Detroit and lived in the area most of her life, except for two years in NYC. She has lived in Huntington Woods for 43 years.

Wendy worked as a writer/producer in a variety of media for more than 50 years, including radio and television news, marketing and public relations, video production, and training.

After more than 20 years as a cat lady, Wendy took in her late cousin's sweet 11-year-old dog three years ago at the start of the pandemic. She says that she and Annabelle are now bonded.

BETH ROBINSON

Beth has had a dual career as a writer and a Jewish communal professional and volunteer. She served as director of the 1990 and 1998 Detroit Maccabi Games, Maccabi Club board member and delegation head, administrator at Congregation Beth Achim and Temple Emanu-El, and director of the Book Fair and Film Festival at the J before coming to Jewish Senior Life as Director of FRIENDS.

As a writer, she has written advertising, marketing, and informational and instructional materials for clients such as

HAP, Johnson & Johnson, Jeep, Dodge, and Citibank. She has written for publications including *Michigan Jewish History*, a publication of the Jewish Historical Society of Michigan, *The Oakland Press*, *Detroit Metro Times*, the *Jewish News*, and *The New York Times*.

Recently, Beth has turned her focus to ghostwriting, coaching, and editing, publishing an anthology titled *The Epiphanies Project: Twenty Personal Revelations*, in 2021.

JO ROSEN

In 2018, Jo joined the executive team of Jewish Senior Life as Director of Development. Prior to this position, she worked in development for over 20 years raising funds for two non-profits, the American Technion Society and the American Cancer Society.

Jo is committed to raising funds that support programs and projects for the residents on both campuses at JSL. Her weekly newsletter from the development department promotes healthy aging and the happy and healthy lives and relationships our residents have with each other and our staff.

Jo is passionate about art, writing, and making magical moments during meetings with residents and volunteers. She's delighted to publicize the programs and services JSL offers that encourage our greater Detroit community to volunteer and live with us. When not working, she loves spending time with her friends, family, husband, children, and grandchildren as well as cooking, making art, listening to podcasts, attending lectures and concerts, and her weeknight passion, *Jeopardy*.

PHYLLIS SCHWARTZ

After a short teaching career, Phyllis Schwartz earned a MSW and worked at Jewish Family Service as a clinical social worker until retirement. She's now part of the enrichment team at Jewish

Hospice and Chaplaincy Network's legacy book project. She is a writer and interviewer for the Legacy Enrichment program, which documents family stories to create books that are gifts for future generations.

DR. CHARLES SILOW

Charles Silow, PhD, is a clinical psychologist and the Director of the Program for Holocaust Survivors and Families of Jewish Senior Life. The program conducts psychosocial programs for the Holocaust survivor community of Detroit, which includes support groups and counseling sessions; Café Europa, a monthly socialization program; friendly visitor programs; and Portraits of Honor: Our Michigan Holocaust Survivors (found at portraitsofhonor.org), a photographic/oral history project which includes photographs and interviews with more than 550 survivors. Portraits of Honor is housed at the Holocaust Center in Farmington Hills.

Dr. Silow is the founder and current co-President of Children of Holocaust Survivors Association in Michigan (CHAIM), Detroit's second-generation organization which began in 1979.

JON LYBECK

Photography is his chosen language for storytelling. He sees the world not just as it appears but as a tapestry of emotions, moments, and tales waiting to be shared. Every photograph he takes is a chapter in a larger narrative, whether it's the wrinkled hands of an elderly artisan, the bustling streets of a foreign market, or the serenity of a remote landscape. He strives to capture the essence and spirit of the places and people he encounters.

JEWISH SENIOR LIFE OF METROPOLITAN DETROIT

Jewish Senior Life of Metropolitan Detroit is far more than a place to live. It's six beautiful residences in two vibrant communities in southeast Michigan where bonds of friendship are built or renewed and passions are pursued. It's where residents actively engage with one another and, as a result, remain active in mind, body, and spirit. And it's where creative programs and services extend spiritual, social, and cultural values of the Jewish tradition to residents, families, and community members. JSL is a place where older adults can embrace life and community in a secure and supportive environment.

JSL is proud to provide inclusive residential communities. We welcome all people without regard to race, color, national origin, religion, disability, gender, sex, sexual orientation, gender identity, age, familial status, and marital status.

FRIENDS OF JEWISH SENIOR LIFE

Don't Write Me Off! is a project of FRIENDS of Jewish Senior Life, the support arm of Jewish Senior Life of Metropolitan Detroit, is dedicated to enhancing the quality of life for older adults in the Metropolitan Detroit community by engaging residents and community members in volunteerism, outreach, and fundraising in accordance with Jewish values, while providing funding to support diverse programming.

Made in the USA
Columbia, SC
12 November 2023